JONAH

The Reluctant Prophet

JONAH
The Reluctant Prophet

By

WILLIAM L. BANKS

MOODY PRESS
CHICAGO

ISBN: 0-8024-2032-X

Printed in the United States of America

CONTENTS

5

Introduction

THE CHIEF CHARACTER of this story is Jonah, the son of Amittai. There are those who deny such a person ever existed, but the evidence for a historical Jonah weighs heavily against them. First of all, the book itself gives no basis for rejecting its historicity. Second, there is mention of a Jonah, the son of Amittai, in II Kings 14:25:

> He restored the coast of Israel from the entering of Hamath unto the sea of the plain, according to the word of the LORD God of Israel, which he spake by the hand of his servant Jonah, the son of Amittai, the prophet, which was of Gath-hepher.

Jonah's prediction of Israel's success against Syria was fulfilled in the reign of Jeroboam II, who ruled from approximately 793 B.C. to 753 B.C. It is not certain whether the prophet lived before or during Jeroboam's reign. Jonah was from the town of Gath-hepher, which means, literally, "wine press of the well." This town was in Galilee, and was only a few miles north of Nazareth. The angry

Pharisees probably overlooked this, when they said to Nicodemus, "Art thou also of Galilee? Search, and look: for out of Galilee ariseth no prophet."

Third, there is a Hebrew tradition which claims that the widow of Zarephath was the mother of Jonah. It is said that she called her child the "son of truth," because Elijah the prophet had spoken truth to her about the child.

Fourth, the Lord Jesus Christ obviously believed that such a person as Jonah lived.

> But he answered and said unto them, An evil and adulterous generation seeketh after a sign; and there shall no sign be given to it, but the sign of the prophet Jonas: For as Jonas was three days and three nights in the whale's belly; so shall the Son of man be three days and three nights in the heart of the earth. The men of Nineveh shall rise in judgment with this generation, and shall condemn it: because they repented at the preaching of Jonas; and, behold, a greater than Jonas is here (Matt. 12:39-41).

Thus denials of a historical Jonah raise more questions than are answered. Nothing is gained by the attempt to make Jonah a fictional character. We approach the study of this book, then, believing it is an historical account.

Outline

THE FIRST COMMISSION—1:1—2:10

I. Commission Given (1:1-2)
II. Disobedience (1:3)
III. Consequence of Disobedience (1:4-16)
    A. Caught in Storm (1:4-6)
    B. Found Guilty (1:7)
    C. Thrown Overboard (1:8-16)
IV. Deliverance Accomplished (1:17—2:10)
    A. Prepared Fish (1:17—2:10)
    B. Jonah's Prayer (2:1-9)
    C. God's Direction (2:10)

THE SECOND COMMISSION—3:1—4:11

I. Commission Renewed (3:1-2)
II. Obedience (3:3-4)
III. Consequence of Obedience (3:5-10)
    A. Repentance (3:5-9)
    B. Deliverance (3:10)
IV. Displeasure Manifested (4:1-11)
    A. Anger Expressed (4:1-4)
    B. Reproof Prepared (4:5-9)
    C. Lesson Taught (4:10-11)

PART I

The First Commission

CHAPTER 1

COMMISSION GIVEN
(1:1-2)

Now the word of the Lord came unto Jonah the son of Amittai, saying, Arise, go to Nineveh, that great city, and cry against it; for their wickedness is come up before me.

The book of Jonah is not the only book in the Bible that begins with the word *now*. Judges, Ruth, I Samuel, Esther, and Ezekiel also begin this way. Evidently no antecedent is required, although beginning a narrative with the word *now* usually indicates something preceded what is being related. Here the word of the Lord breaks into Jonah's life. Nothing is said about his birth or previous ministry. Nor are we told in what manner the word of the Lord came to him, or whether he had a dream, a vision, or heard a voice. God has used a variety of methods to call men into service and to reveal unto them His will. Such variety is seen in the calling of Abraham, Joseph, Moses, Samuel, Isaiah, Amos, Daniel, Ezekiel, the twelve disciples, and Paul. However God called, we may rest assured Jonah received the message.

The name Jonah means "dove," and expresses beauty, flight, gentleness, mildness, harmlessness, mourning, or peace. When children were named after birds and beasts, it was done in hope that some good characteristic of the animal might be demonstrated in the life of the one so named.

As for Jonah, his name might indicate he moaned and mourned over what he considered a danger to his people and to the cause of God. The word *Amittai* comes from the same Hebrew root which gives us the word *amen*. When you say amen to something, you confirm or support it. It is like saying, "That's the truth!" or "So be it." Thus, Jonah, son of Amittai, means "mourning dove, son of truth."

The words *arise, go,* and *cry* are imperatives and signify the urgency and authority of God's command. The prophet was told in no uncertain terms what he must do. He was to stand up, to go, and to proclaim God's message against the great city of Nineveh. The city of Nineveh is first mentioned in Genesis 10:11. During much of Assyria's history, it was the capital of Assyria (present-day Iraq), and was located on the east, or right, bank of the Tigris River. Assyria was Israel's constant enemy, and the command given to Jonah was at once unwelcome and distasteful.

The people of Nineveh were arrogant, haughty, proud of their achievements. It was indeed a great city, but it was sinking in corruption. The prophet Nahum called it a bloody city, full of fraud, lies, robbery, sensuousness, violence, witchcraft, and idolatry. Assyria's soldiers were noted for their brutality and cruelty. Nineveh's wickedness was known to God, and He was concerned.

The knowledge of man's wickedness on earth ascends to heaven like smoke rising in the air. Multitudes seem totally unaware that their sins are known to God. What God said of Nineveh He had spoken centuries earlier in regard to the twin cities of Sodom and Gomorrah. Their corrupt practice of homosexuality rose up as a stench in His nostrils. God informed Abraham that the cry of Sodom and Gomorrah was great, and said, ". . . their sin is very grievous and the cry of it is come unto me."

Today, the need for missionary activity is still great, for all men continue to sin, and all are falling short of God's glory even now!

Unfortunately, some people in America are blinded by economic prosperity, material possessions, a high standard of living, church membership, and scientific achievements. They think that all is well. However, all is not well. We see a constant increase in crime, divorce, immorality, racial strife, and venereal disease, and in the use of tobacco and alcoholic beverages. The evil on this earth rises as a foul odor to heaven. Evil men everywhere wax worse and worse.

This is why it is necessary for the church to hear anew the voice of God commanding, "Go!" Christians need to go forth and tell present-day Ninevites that the wages of sin is death but that the gift of God is eternal life through Jesus Christ our Lord.

CHAPTER 2

DISOBEDIENCE

(1:3)

But Jonah rose up to flee unto Tarshish from the presence of the LORD, and went down to Joppa; and he found a ship going to Tarshish: so he paid the fare thereof and went down into it, to go with them unto Tarshish from the presence of the LORD.

Having heard the word of the Lord, Jonah's immediate reaction was one of rebellion and disobedience. He substituted his own will for God's will, and he rose up to flee. His mind was made up and his destination chosen; he was going to Tarshish. Scholars are not positive of the exact location of this city. Some have suggested Tarsus, the birthplace of the Apostle Paul, located in the southeastern part of modern Turkey. Some have suggested Italy or the coast of North Africa. Still others believe Tarshish was a commercial port on the southwest coast of Spain.

17

Tarshish is depicted in Old Testament scriptures as a great commercial city, probably a Phoenician colony which traded heavily with Tyre. It is described as rich in gold and silver, and owning many ships. And it was far away from Nineveh!

One wonders what gave birth to this rebellion and disobedience. Was it hatred for the Ninevites? Did he fear that they might obey the word of the Lord, repent, and be saved? It is not until chapter 4, verse 2, that light is shed upon Jonah's motive for disobeying the Lord. The text before us does not seek to explain his motives.

Jonah rebelled in his heart and this spiritual rebellion resulted in physical activity with this purpose: to flee from the presence of the Lord. This desire to flee from God's presence by no means indicates that Jonah did not believe that Jehovah was omnipresent. David had written earlier: "Whither shall I go from thy spirit? or whither shall I flee from thy presence?" (Ps. 139:7).

Jonah believed this. He knew that the Lord was not like the gods whose influence and power, in the conception of their worshipers, did not extend beyond the boundaries of a given area. Jonah thought that running away to a distant place would make him physically unable to discharge his commission. Surely being two thousand miles away from Nineveh would mean that the Lord would have to get somebody else! Flight was to be Jonah's way of withdrawing from the service of God.

The many verbs of action in verse 3 indicate that Jonah's decision was no momentary whim or passing fancy. He rose up to flee, went down to Joppa (modern-day Jaffa, a seaport town on the coast of Israel adjacent to Tel-Aviv), found a ship, paid the fare, and went down into the boat. These deliberate acts demonstrate Jonah's determined effort to avoid obeying the Lord.

Attempting to run away from God's will is like fleeing light and falling into darkness, relinquishing wealth and welcoming poverty, or disdaining wisdom in order to wallow in ignorance. Running away from God's will is like abandoning joy and meeting sorrow, or giving up peace and order for chaos and confusion. Each step Jonah took along the course of self-will carried him further away from God.

Just as Jonah was actively rebellious, so ought Christians to be actively obedient. The battle against sin is not for the weak, the anemic, the spineless, and senile. We are constantly called upon to fight (I Tim. 6:12), flee (I Cor. 6:18), follow (John 12:26), give (II Cor. 9:7), hold fast (I Thess. 5:21), lay hold of (Heb. 6:18), pray (I Thess. 5:17), press on (Phil. 3:14), put on and put off (Eph. 4:22, 24), run (I Cor. 9:24), sing

(Ps. 30:4), stir up (II Tim. 1:6), study (II Tim. 2:15), strive (Luke 13:24), wait (Isa. 40:31), walk (Deut. 13:4), watch (Mark 13:33), and wrestle (Eph. 6:12). These and many more verbs of action and motion requiring energy, power, and force are used to express Christian obedience in action.

The Hebrew verb translated as "found" has, in this text, the connotation of unexpectedness, so that it could be said that Jonah happened upon the ship. Someone has said, "When a person decides to run from the Lord, Satan always provides complete transportation facilities." It seems that whenever we decide to do wrong the devil helps us. However, we should not put the blame on Satan, for he simply encourages us to do what our hearts already desire.

Something else is to be seen in Jonah's actions. His commission and subsequent rebellion typify the nation Israel. It was God's purpose that Israel should make Him known to all nations and people as the true and living God. Israel neglected to do this and because of her disobedience has been set aside temporarily. At a future time Israel's eyes will be opened and the Jews will accept Jesus as the Christ and fulfill her great missionary calling to the world.

To a high degree the present-day church has

missed its calling. Our rebellion against God in failing to spread the Gospel of Jesus Christ is perhaps not yet as bold and deliberate as Jonah's way, but is rather more subtle. We are busy, but not with the Lord's business. Many of our churches have become obsessed with the physical and the temporal, and the materialistic spirit has been nourished and fed at the expense of the cause of missions.

Someone once asked an artist to paint a picture of a decaying church. When the work was completed many of those who viewed it were astonished. They had expected to see a picture of an old, crumbling, dilapidated ruin. Instead, the artist had drawn a magnificent edifice. Through the open doors could be seen the richly carved furniture, the splendid organ, and the beautiful stained glass windows. Within the entrance was an elaborately designed offering plate, above which hung a box designated "Foreign Missions." And directly above the slot through which money was to go, was a huge cobweb!

CHAPTER 3

CONSEQUENCE OF DISOBEDIENCE
(1:4-16)

A. *Caught in Storm* (1:4-6)

But the LORD sent out a great wind into the sea, and there was a mighty tempest in the sea, so that the ship was like to be broken. Then the mariners were afraid, and cried every man unto his god, and cast forth the wares that were in the ship into the sea, to lighten it of them. But Jonah was gone down into the sides of the ship; and he lay, and was fast asleep. So the shipmaster came to him, and said unto him, What meanest thou, O sleeper? arise, call upon thy God, if so be that God will think upon us, that we perish not.

Some of God's children are not willing to acknowledge that they bring trouble upon themselves. Others are unaware that their misery is self-made. There is a difference between the storms of life which befall the man out of God's will and the tempests which assail the man who is directly in the Lord's will.

Peter touched upon this when he wrote, "If ye be reproached for the name of Christ, happy are ye; for the Spirit of glory and of God resteth upon you: on their part he is evil spoken of, but on your part he is glorified. But let none of you suffer as a murderer, or as a thief, or as an evildoer, or as a busybody in other men's matters. Yet if any man suffer as a Christian, let him not be ashamed; but let him glorify God on this behalf" (I Peter 4:14-16).

Rebellion never escapes God's notice, and it is foolish for men to think they can resist God's will with impunity. Sometimes a Christian may presumptuously violate God's will and then continue unrepentant. Time may roll by, perhaps even a year may pass, but eventually the voice of God will be heard announcing, "Thou art the man." The Lord may let a man go to a certain point before He steps in, but when He *does* move, He moves with no uncertainty. He wasted no time with Jonah, but sent out a great wind to stir up the sea.

This was no ordinary storm. The word translated "sent out" comes from a verb meaning "hurl" or "cast." It is used in I Samuel 18:11, where we read that Saul cast a javelin at David. This verb indicates force and power, and points out that the tempest was a furious one. The ship was in danger of being wrecked, and the experienced seamen were frightened.

It is interesting to note that the word translated "mariners" is similar to the Hebrew noun which means "salt." The connection is obvious; colloquially, a sailor is sometimes called a salt.

The first reaction of the sailors was to pray, a not uncommon reaction to danger. The only time some people will pray is when they are in trouble and fear strikes them. But notice that the sailors directed their prayers to idols! Since the sailors prayed to more than one god, this would indicate either a difference in their nationality or in their place of birth. Even if all of them had been Phoenicians, it was quite possible for their prayers to be directed to more than one god, for the Phoenicians were polytheistic.

Polytheism exists today, and multitudes are wasting time, energy, and money worshiping various gods. It may sound harsh, and there are those who rebel at the thought, but biblical Christianity claims that the only true and living God is the God and Father of Jesus Christ.

The Old Testament clearly teaches that Jehovah, God of Israel, is alone the true God: "I am the LORD, and there is none else, there is no God beside me" (Isa. 45:5). In the New Testament the Apostle Paul announced to the Ephesian believers that before their conversion they were "without Christ, being aliens from the commonwealth of Israel, and strangers from the covenants of promise, having no hope, and without God in the world" (Eph. 2:12). In another place he stated: "The things which the Gentiles sacrifice, they sacrifice to devils [demons], and not to God" (I Cor. 10:20).

Such language as this means that apart from the God of the Bible and apart from Christ there is no hope for mankind. This is an unpleasant and unacceptable statement for many in this age of broadmindedness, religious tolerance, and increasing acceptance of universalism. Nonetheless, such a statement is true, and ought to stir the heart of every true saint!

To save the ship from sinking, the sailors threw the wares overboard. The word translated "wares" also means "article, utensil, vessel." Some commentators seem to be uncertain whether the cargo itself was thrown overboard or just the tackling and equipment. The word is used over three hundred times in the Old Testament and is variously translated "armor, bag, carriage, garment, jewel, instrument, sack, stuff, thing, tool, vessel, weapon." Such usage would seem to suggest that the Hebrew word includes cargo and should not be restricted to the tackling and gear.

In the Greek Old Testament, commonly called the Septuagint, this verse speaks of a casting out or throwing overboard. This nautical term for jettisoning refers to the literal "throwing out" of a ship's cargo in order to save the ship. The same word is used in Acts 27:18, and Luke's account of the ship in the storm strengthens our position that the cargo on Jonah's ship was thrown overboard.

A study of the actions taken by the experienced seamen in Acts 27 will show the order of importance. First of all, they brought aboard, with some difficulty, the dinghy or small boat usually towed behind. Second, they undergirded the ship. Then the gear was lowered. The King James Version states that they "strake sail," but this is better translated "they lowered the gear," which means that a floating anchor was dropped, or, better still, the yard with the sail attached to it was lowered.

The fourth step taken for safety's sake was to jettison the cargo. Somewhat later the men discovered that something more drastic would have to be done, and this time the spare gear and tackling equipment were thrown overboard. Because of these actions taken in Acts 27, it seems reasonable to infer that the men in Jonah's ship got rid of their cargo first, and then—and only when it was absolutely necessary—they cut loose the gear and rigging equipment.

The efforts of the mariners are typical of men's efforts to solve their problems. We are not willing to acknowledge that the root of our trouble is sin. We have failed to deal with the sin which is concealed within the inner recesses of the human heart and have treated only the symptoms. We are casting overboard the ware and cargo, but the storm continues to rage because sin continues to rule in the hearts of those aboard the ship of life. Nothing weighs a man down as heavily as the burden of sin.

Before the storm broke, Jonah, dead tired, had found some inner recess in a lower part of the ship and had fallen asleep. This was no ordinary sleep, but rather a deep heavy sleep. It was like the deep sleep God caused to fall upon Adam before creating Eve from his rib, or like the deep sleep of Sisera when Jael drove a tent peg through his temple. And the same word tells us of King Saul's sound sleep—so sound that he could have lost his life— on the occasion when David took only the spear and cruse of water from him (I Sam. 26:12). Surely Jonah's continued sleeping in the midst of a terrific storm likewise indicates an unusually sound sleep—a sign of something supernatural.

The word for "shipmaster" is *chief-sailor*. Literally, the word for "sailor" is *rope-puller*, or *rope-twister*. Thus, it was the chief of the rope-pullers who approached the sleeping Jonah and was as-

tonished to find Jonah asleep. After all, how could
anyone sleep at a time like this?

"What do you mean by sleeping? Get up, **and
pray to** your god! Perhaps the god will give **a
thought** to us, that we do not perish!" The word
god is not capitalized. This is because the captain
was a heathen, as were the rest of his crew. He had
no idea that Jonah's God was the true and living
God, the one and only Ruler of the world.

It would be more in keeping with his character
as a heathen to say that he felt all gods were needed
in such a time of peril. The others had prayed, yet
the storm had not abated. Possibly Jonah's god
might be the one to tip the balance of mercy in
their favor. United we stay afloat, divided we are
wrecked, and perish.

Perhaps the shipmaster's voice expressed indignation as he reproached Jonah for not cooperating
to win mercy from the gods. The record does not
tell whether Jonah prayed then or not, but we do
read that the crew decided to take further action.

B. *Found Guilty* (1:7)

And they said every one to his fellow, Come, and
let us cast lots, that we may know for whose cause
this evil is upon us. So they cast lots, and the lot
fell upon Jonah.

The storm did not cease; rather it increased in —

intensity. The men were at their wits' end when it occurred to them that this sudden violent tempest was the result or expression of the gods' anger with someone on board. Unless that guilty person was discovered, all would perish. The ancients believed that when evil befell a man it was the natural consequence of that man's own wickedness. This was the viewpoint of Job's comforters. The Jews felt this way about the Galileans whose blood Pilate had mingled with their sacrifices (Luke 13:1-2), and they felt the same way about the eighteen upon whom the tower of Siloam fell (Luke 13:4). And such was the opinion of the natives of Melita when they saw a viper fasten itself to Paul's hand (Acts 28:4).

We know today that this concept is fallacious. Many people literally get away with murder; we never see nor hear of anything bad happening to them. On the other hand, there are those saints who suffer for no apparent reason.

While the ancients were wrong in assuming that any and every evil which came to a man was the result of his sin, yet it would appear that they were aware of something which has escaped most moderns. They recognized a relationship between man's sin and natural calamity. When floods, earthquakes, hurricanes, volcanic eruptions, mountain slides, and other natural calamities occur today, seldom do we hear anyone suggest any connection with sin.

Some men curse God; some satisfy themselves with the scientific explanation of the event; others simply resign themselves to it. Naturally we cannot directly pinpoint sins and relate them to natural catastrophes, but we do well to remember that such is the seriousness of sin that nature has been—and is—affected. (See II Chron. 7:13-14.)

What was the significance behind the casting of lots? The corresponding Arabic word means "stones, pebbles, stony place." Stones, pebbles, dice, colored balls, pieces of wood of different lengths, and so on, were used. Because men of old believed that the will of the powers which ruled over man's destiny could be known in this way, it was a common practice to cast lots for important decisions. In this way serious disputes were often settled.

We find in the Bible several references to the use of the lot. For instance in Proverbs 16:33 we read, "The lot is cast into the lap; but the whole disposing thereof is of the LORD." Or, as someone else has put it, "Man throws the dice, but God makes the spots come up." Men regarded the outcome of the lots as supernatural.

Lots were cast at Shiloh by Joshua in order that the land might be divided among the remaining

seven tribes of the children of Israel (Joshua 18:
10). But most often lots were cast in order to assign to service or duty or punishment. The last
mention made of casting lots is found in Acts 1:
26, where we read about the choosing of someone
to take the place of Judas. After the day of Pente-
cost this method of finding God's will was no longer used. The Holy Spirit, who now indwells all
believers, teaches them and guides them into truth.
The throne of God is accessible through the blood
of Jesus Christ, and we have confidence that God
hears and answers our prayers.

We find God's will expressed in the Bible, but
unfortunately some people handle the Bible in a
rather superstitious way, almost as if they were casting lots. We are reminded of the story of a man
who would arise each morning and open up his
Bible at random, place his finger on the page, and
whatever verse his finger pointed to he would take
as God's message for him for that day.

One morning his finger fell on Matthew 27:5;
which tells about Judas hanging himself. Somewhat puzzled, he tried again, and turned to Luke
10:37, where he read: "Go, and do thou likewise."
Exasperated, he tried a third time, and his finger
pointed to John 13:27: "That thou doest, do quick-
ly!"

In God's providence, Jonah was discovered as

the culprit. He was the guilty one. You may be
sure that your sins will find you out, and sometimes
in the presence of unbelievers! It is a sad thing
when God exposes the sin of a Christian before the
eyes of the unbelieving world, but it does happen.
It may happen to any Christian who is out of the
will of Christ. The world does not understand that
the Lord chastens His own, and that even exposure
before unbelievers is calculated to benefit the child
of God. Jonah was out of the will of the Lord, and
God had exposed him.

C. *Thrown Overboard* (1:8-16)

Then said they unto him, Tell us, we pray thee,
for whose cause this evil is upon us; What is thine
occupation? and whence comest thou? what is thy
country? and of what people art thou? And he
said unto them, I am an Hebrew; and I fear the
LORD, the God of heaven, which hath made the
sea and the dry land. Then were the men exceedingly afraid, and said unto him, Why hast thou
done this? For the men knew that he fled from the
presence of the LORD, because he had told them.

Then said they unto him, What shall we do
unto thee, that the sea may be calm unto us? for
the sea wrought, and was tempestuous. And he
said unto them, Take me up, and cast me forth
into the sea; so shall the sea be calm unto you:
for I know that for my sake this great tempest is
upon you. Nevertheless the men rowed hard to

bring it to the land; but they could not: for the sea wrought, and was tempestuous against them. Wherefore they cried unto the Lord, and said, We beseech thee, O Lord, we beseech thee, let us not perish for this man's life, and lay not upon us innocent blood: for thou, O Lord, hast done as it pleased thee. So they took up Jonah, and cast him forth into the sea: and the sea ceased from her raging. Then the men feared the Lord exceedingly, and offered a sacrifice unto the Lord, and made vows.

From the viewpoint of the sailors it was the gods, or a god, who had exposed the guilty man, the man responsible for the storm. Naturally, they wanted to know more about him, and they asked a series of pertinent questions. Their first question was "Tell us, on whose account has this evil come upon us?" In view of the fact that they had just cast lots and the casting of the lot pointed to Jonah as the guilty one, this question would seem superfluous. But Jonah's answer would help the crew decide the next step.

It was not that the men doubted the lot. But if Jonah would confess his guilt with his own words, if he himself would acknowledge it, the lot would be confirmed. So this first question was important and, once asked, it was only natural for other questions to follow.

"What is your occupation?" Perhaps they sus-
pected Jonah's occupation was disreputable and
displeasing to the gods, and that this had been the
reason for the gods' wrath. On the other hand, the
question could be interpreted, "What is your business on this ship now? Why are you taking this
trip?"

As the crew continued its pointed questioning,
they asked, "Whence do you come? What is your
country? and of what people are you?" Jonah answered the last question first by saying to them, "I
am a Hebrew." In the Old Testament the term
"Hebrew" was used whenever an Israelite described
himself to a foreigner or heathen. In the New
Testament it was used of those Jews who spoke Hebrew and Aramaic, in contrast to the Jews who
spoke Greek, these latter being called Hellenists.

The term "Israelite" is much more restricted
than the term "Hebrew" and, when used in the
Old Testament pertained to a descendant of Israel,
that is, Jacob. An Israelite belonged to a nation
with a special relationship to God, and was an in-
heritor of God's promises to the nation Israel. The
term "Jew" originally signified one who belonged
to the tribe of Judah or to the kingdom of Judah,
which was made up of the descendants of two sons
of Jacob, Judah and Benjamin. Later the term was
applied to all who had returned from the captivity,

including proselytes. In time, the religious significance increased, so that the term "Jew" was used
to distinguish one who practiced Judaism from a
Gentile or a Greek.

We see that the lines cannot be too clearly
drawn, but it might help to consider the term "Hebrew" as referring to language, "Israelite" as referring to nationality, and "Jew" to religion.

Now Jonah was very frank and open with his
interrogators. Concerning his faith as a Hebrew
he said: "I fear the LORD, the God of heaven, who
made the sea and the dry land." Does it sound
strange that a man actively disobeying the Lord
should make such a profession as this? He did not
claim to be either innocent or righteous, but rather
spoke of his relationship with God. The fear of the
Lord is not a servile, cringing type of fear but involves the idea of worship. It means reverential
awe, trust, and respect. This was the concept Jonah wanted known. Furthermore, His God was
the God of heaven, who made both the sea and the
dry land. For Jonah to answer the crew in this
manner indicated some measure of self-righteous-
ness. As far as he was concerned, he had done the
right thing in running away, and the act in itself
in no way hindered him from announcing, "I
fear the Lord, . . ."

Now if Jonah's claims were true, then it was Jo-

nah's God who had sent the storm. How then
could Jonah rebel against such a god? The sailors
were amazed by what Jonah told them. It was as
if they said, "Jonah, if your god is the god of
heaven, sea, and land, how could you dare disobey
him?" The men recoiled in horror at the sheer
folly of the idea. "What is this you've done!" they
exclaimed. They were not probing into Jonah's
past to discover what awful crime had been com-
mitted that would cause a god to pursue him.
Rather, this was an exclamation of horror!

Since Jonah was the prophet of this god, it was
more than likely that Jonah knew what his god desired. So the men asked, "What shall we do to you,
that the sea may calm down for us?" The storm's
intensity had increased. The Hebrew says literally: "For the sea [is] growing and storming." This
means that, as they talked, the sea grew more and
more tempestuous. The two active participles,
"growing" and "storming," denote a continuous
progressive action. So all the time Jonah and the
crew were talking the storm grew worse.

Jonah then answered, "Take me up, and cast me
forth into the sea." What could have been in Jonah's mind at the time? What does his command
to the sailors indicate? The words "then the sea
will quiet down for you" show that Jonah was concerned about the welfare of the crew. He knew

that the storm had been sent by God because of his disobedience, and he was not willing that the sailors should die because of his folly.

But was the concern about the crew the only motivation for Jonah's request that he be cast into the ocean? Sometimes adverse conditions and perilous situations stiffen a man's resistance to the will of God. In the case of Pharaoh, he hardened his heart. At other times painful vicissitudes soften the heart and a man becomes more amenable to the will of God, and more receptive to His workings.

If the tempest served to harden Jonah's will, it meant that Jonah was willing to perish rather than to preach. Bigotry can become so ingrained in the human personality that not even the threat of physical harm or punishment will eradicate it, nor will arguments and appeals to reason. Those who have had experience with race bigots know that logic and reason and common sense are thrown to the wind, and the arguments against race hatred accomplish little.

Even though Jonah asked the crew to throw him overboard, they were reluctant to do so. Without doubt, the intensity of the storm, the falling of the lot upon Jonah, and Jonah's subsequent confession all impressed the sailors, but it is unlikely that they were restrained from throwing Jonah overboard because of a feeling of mercy toward him.

It would be more in keeping with their characters to attribute their reluctance to fear, and not to mercy. They may have hesitated to lay hold of a man after whom a god would chase and raise such a tempest. They evidently believed that Jonah was a chosen servant of a powerful god. Besides, how could the sailors know for certain that their actions would please Jonah's god? They probably felt that the proper thing to do, the thing which would please Jonah's god, would be to take Jonah back to the land.

The word translated "bring" comes from a verb meaning "to turn back or return." The mariners intended to return Jonah to the land; this might be the very thing the god desired! But they could not do it, no matter how hard they rowed; and they did row hard because the word translated "rowed" comes from a verb meaning "to dig." The idea of digging the oars into the water is a metaphor which suggests strenuous effort. Finally, the fact that the men were unsuccessful and the fact that the tempest increased in fury showed that it was not God's intention that Jonah be returned to dry land. At least, not yet.

The men saw that no headway was being made against the storm, so they began to pray earnestly to Jonah's god. They were now increasingly concerned about their own welfare. If Jonah was to be disposed of, they wanted to be sure it was all right with Jonah's god.

We doubt that the crew's reluctance to sacrifice Jonah was a sign of conversion. They were frightened. If such a god pursued a disobedient prophet, what might he do to these sailors who had never even prayed to him before? "If the righteous scarcely be saved, where shall the ungodly and the sinner appear?" And, more important, what would such a god do to those who would throw his servant overboard?

Their prayer contained two requests. The first was "Let us not perish," and its earnestness is noted by the use of the word *beseech* twice. Believing that the sea would soon be Jonah's watery grave, they did not want to perish for taking his life.

Their second request was "Lay not upon us innocent blood." This does not mean that the crew regarded Jonah as innocent or clear of any charge. They wanted Jonah's god to know that they would not be guilty of willful murder. The life is in the blood, and the shedding of man's blood meant taking his life. They reasoned, "Surely Jonah's god cannot hold us responsible!" After all, Jonah had come to the ship of his own free will, on his own initiative and his god had stirred up the storm.

Besides, they had had no control over the lot which fell upon Jonah, and the runaway prophet himself had suggested being thrown overboard. Therefore they politely informed the Lord that they had no control over these factors. The circumstances leading to the present predicament were not of their own choosing but, rather, Jonah's god had done as it pleased him.

Having prayed to Jonah's god, the men lifted Jonah up and hurled him into the ocean. Since Jonah had made up his mind to die, he offered no resistance. Certainly he had been concerned about the lives of the crewmen, but his dominant emotion was his spirit of rebellion.

It probably never entered into his mind to jump overboard and commit suicide. This would have spared the sailors their consternation and fear. But the Hebrews had a horror of suicide, and very few suicides are recorded in the Bible.

The first suicide is that of the strong man, Samson. Though blind, he dislodged the pillars of the house and it fell upon him, and about three thousand Philistines who were upon the roof were killed. The defeated Saul thrust himself through with a sword when he was unsuccessful in getting his armor-bearer to do it. And the armor-bearer, realizing the tragedy of the situation, likewise fell upon his sword and died with Saul. Ahithophel hanged himself, and Zimri, fifth king of Israel, went into the palace and burned it down upon his own head. And Judas Iscariot hanged himself after betraying our Lord.

When rebellious Jonah was thrown into the water, the sea became calm and ceased its raging and whirling. This demonstrated to the mariners that Jonah had been at fault. This incident reminds us of the time when the Lord Jesus rebuked the wind and said to the stormy sea of Galilee, "Peace, be still." As He muzzled the storm, He demonstrated that He was the Ruler of all nature, who "maketh the storm a calm, so that the waves thereof are still" (Ps. 107:29).

This is the last we hear of the sailors. Since their cargo had been thrown overboard earlier, and the ocean was now calm, we might assume that they returned to port. Once in port, they spread the news of the sudden calming of the wild ocean after Jonah was thrown overboard, and expressed themselves as being sure he had drowned.

But what was the total effect of this experience upon these men? Did it lead to their conversion? Did these mariners accept Jonah's God and become Jonah's first converts? Surely many astounding things had happened since they left port! However, we would not claim that this crew constituted Jonah's first missionary converts. The fear they showed could have been only temporary, lacking true piety. Fear is a great inventor. Many things are done and many vows are made under stress and strain which, when conditions become more favorable, are soon forgotten. This characteristic of human nature creates doubt in our minds that these men abandoned their own gods to fully serve Jehovah, the God of Jonah and Israel.

As for the sacrifice mentioned in verse 16, it is quite possible that some animals suitable for sacrificial purposes had been retained and not jettisoned during the storm. Perhaps they felt the sacrifice they offered was not sufficient, for they promised to do more upon reaching dry land safely. We read that they "made vows." But even the fact that they offered a sacrifice unto the Lord is not conclusive proof that they were converted. We are not convinced that these men abandoned their gods for the God of Jonah. They were influenced by unusual events, and simply reacted in ways we should regard as natural and expedient.

CHAPTER 4

DELIVERANCE ACCOMPLISHED
(1:17—2:10)

A. *Prepared Fish* (1:17)

Now the Lord had prepared a great fish to swallow up Jonah. And Jonah was in the belly of the fish three days and three nights.

In the Hebrew Bible this is the first verse of chapter 2. At this point the book of Jonah has incurred the full wrath and ridicule of naturalists, humanists, and rationalists. Those who reject the Bible as God's Word desire to eliminate all talk about the supernatural. Accordingly, some say that the story of Jonah is a myth, a folk tale not to be taken seriously or literally. Others say that it is poetry and should not be dealt with as prose. Some suggest that the whole story was but a dream or vision.

Another effort to get rid of the supernatural element suggests that Jonah either landed atop a living fish or upon the floating dead carcass of a whale. Another suggestion is that there was a ship whose name was "The Fish" which happened by and picked Jonah out of the ocean.

There are many miracles mentioned in the Bible: Enoch translated, Lot's wife turned to a pillar of salt, a bush burned but not consumed, a donkey made to speak, plagues sent, the Red Sea divided, the Jordan River held up, manna sent from heaven, quails supplied by God, water made to gush from a rock, the sun made to stand still, Isaac born in old age, an axhead made to float upon water, food supplied by a raven, oil multiplied, visions given, dreams interpreted, jaws of hungry lions locked, and the dead brought to life again.

In the New Testament it is recorded that water was turned into wine, sight was given to the blind, deaf ears were unstopped, tongues were loosed, water was walked upon, minds were restored, bread and fish were multiplied, demons were cast out, the lame were made to walk, men spoke in tongues, and the dead were raised.

If one miracle can be rejected, why not all? Why then is this miracle in Jonah so bitterly assailed? Is it because it so beautifully typifies or prefigures the death, burial, and resurrection of our Lord and Saviour Jesus Christ?

Direct divine intervention is one of the chief characteristics of the book of Jonah. Notice the words "God prepared." The word translated "prepared" means also "to count, appoint, assign, designate, determine, number, ordain, reckon, set apart." We are impressed when we read elsewhere in the book of Jonah that the Lord also prepared a plant to shade Jonah; then He prepared a worm to eat and destroy the plant and, finally, He prepared an east wind to blow upon Jonah.

The word *prepare* includes the idea of creation. But whether or not a special fish already existed for this occasion, a miracle was performed. God saw to it that this creature of the deep could and would do exactly what He wanted done.

The word *fish* here is a generic term. It is not specific; we do not know the species or the exact kind of creature it was. Many believe it was some type of shark, or possibly a sperm whale. In Matthew 12:40, the Greek word translated "whale" is better translated "sea monster" or "great fish," and thus may well include a whale. Although they are scientifically incorrect, people commonly call a whale a fish. And since both the Hebrew Old Testament and the Greek New Testament employ the generic terms, we cannot be certain of the species or exact kind of creature it was.

However, there does appear to be much proof

that it is possible for certain creatures of the deep to swallow a man whole. However, much of the discussion about the narrowness of the throat and the size of the esophagus or gullet is irrelevant and useless. After all, if God prepared such a creature for this special task, it is doubtful if any scientific research in the matter will prove fruitful or beneficial.

One question often asked is whether Jonah actually died at this time. Did he lose his life when suddenly swallowed by this denizen of the deep? Some conservative Bible scholars believe that he died and point out that this best typifies what happened to Christ.

However, a type is a prefigure or foreshadow of the real thing and it should never be unduly pressed. There are many obvious dissimilarities between Christ and Jonah and it would be unwise to so press the issue and violate the purpose of the typology. Most of the second chapter of Jonah discloses his thoughts, prayers, and experiences in the belly of the fish. But no one else in the Bible, having been brought to life again, gives a detailed account of his experience in death. We doubt if Jonah is an exception to this.

In Matthew 12:39-40 Jonah's ordeal is called by our Lord a sign: "An evil and adulterous generation seeketh after a sign; and there shall be no sign given to it, but the sign of the prophet Jonas: for as Jonas was three days and three nights in the whale's belly; so shall the Son of man be three days and three nights in the heart of the earth." It was a sign to Jonah's generation, even as Christ's burial and resurrection were to be a sign to His generation and generations following. Our Lord regarded Jonah as historical. Those who deny the historicity of the book of Jonah suggest:

1. Matthew 12:40 is not genuine, and therefore these words were never actually spoken by Christ.

2. Jesus Christ was of necessity a product of his own time. He simply imbibed the teachings of his time, and therefore, like the other Jews, accepted Jonah as historical.

3. By virtue of the incarnation, Jesus Christ was limited in knowledge. In other words, He did not know any better than to accept Jonah as historical.

Actually these suggestions and others similar to them solve nothing. They serve only to raise unanswerable speculative questions in the mind of the hearer. Unfortunately some have accepted these theories and have come to regard the book of Jonah as nothing more than a myth, an allegory, or a parable. We believe that the experience of Jonah is a remarkable foreshadowing of the burial and resurrection of Jesus Christ. The sign of which our Lord spoke was the real, actual, historical experience of Jonah in the belly of the fish for three days and three nights.

Now what of these three days and three nights? If Jonah stayed this length of time in the belly of the fish, how long did our Lord remain in the tomb? Three days and three nights? If so, this means we should not hold to the deeply entrenched tradition of a Good Friday.

Perhaps the failure to recognize that there was more than one Sabbath during that week is one reason for the acceptance of a Good Friday. We read in John 19:31: "The Jews therefore, because it was the preparation, that the bodies should not remain upon the cross on the sabbath day, (for that sabbath day was an high day,) besought Pilate that their legs might be broken, and that they might be taken away." Notice that this was not the regular weekly sabbath, but "an high day"—the first day of unleavened bread. It indicates that the Lord Jesus died before this great festival began.

The Jews used the expression "day and night" to indicate a full twenty-four hour period. You may recall that in John 11:9, Jesus said, "Are there not twelve hours in the day?" There are twelve hours in the night also. Thus, wherever the phrase "day and night" occurs it speaks of a complete twenty-four-hour period, and three days and three nights would approximate seventy-two hours. For the Hebrew a day and night was from sunset to sunset, which was about seven in the evening to seven the next evening.

Let us assume that the paschal meal was on a Tuesday evening of Holy Week. This in turn would support the belief that Christ was crucified on a Wednesday. Here is the way we believe the week went.

Sunset Wednesday would have heralded the beginning of a new day—in this case, a sabbath day. Because it was the Jewish custom that no work be done on the sabbath, preparations for the burial had to be made before the sabbath began. This is why Joseph of Arimathea and Nicodemus made haste to take down His body that Wednesday afternoon. They wanted to prepare it and bury it before sunset (John 19:42). Sunset Wednesday to sunset Thursday constituted the first day Christ's body remained in the tomb. By Jewish reckoning this was a Thursday and, according to the Scriptures, was a sabbath; not the regular weekly sabbath, but a special sabbath, a high day.

Sunset Thursday to sunset Friday was the second day of burial. According to the Jewish custom this was a Friday. Sunset Friday to sunset Saturday

was the regular weekly sabbath and was the third
day of burial. By Jewish calculation this was a
Saturday. Thus the Lord Jesus remained in the
grave three whole days and nights, approximately
seventy-two hours.

Again, consider the matter from the standpoint
of the sealing of the tomb. Christ was crucified and
buried on the day of preparation for the Passover.
This is plainly taught in John 19:14, 31 and Mark
15:42, at which time Joseph begged for the body.
Sunset of that same day ushered in the special sabbath or high day.

Matthew 27:62 states: "Now the next day, that
followed the day of the preparation, the chief
priests and Pharisees came together unto Pilate."
It was the day after the preparation, that is, it was
sometime during the special sabbath day itself,
that the chief priests and Pharisees came to Pilate
and requested that the tomb be sealed and watched.
At that time the body had lain in the tomb almost
a day. Then the command was given "that the
sepulchre be made sure until the third day." This
meant that the guards would have at least two days
to keep watch. Those who say the crucifixion took
place on Friday ignore these facts. If, as tradition
holds, our Lord died on Friday afternoon and was
resurrected on Sunday morning, then the com-

mand to seal and guard the tomb until the third day would not make much sense.

Again, consider this: For the Jew, sunset Saturday announced the end of the weekly sabbath and the beginning of the first day of a new week. It was at this time that the resurrection of Christ occurred. All four Gospels make it clear that our Lord had risen prior to the coming of the women. When they arrived early that first day of the week they discovered that He was not there. He had been resurrected before their arrival.

> In the *end* of the sabbath, as it *began to dawn* toward the *first day* of the week, came Mary Magdalene and the other Mary to see the sepulchre (Matt. 28:1).

> And when the *sabbath was past,* Mary Magdalene, and Mary the mother of James, and Salome, had bought sweet spices, that they might come and anoint him. And very *early in the morning,* the *first day of the week,* they came unto the sepulchre at the *rising of the sun* (Mark 16:1-2).

> Now upon the first day of the week, *very early in the morning,* they came upon the sepulchre (Luke 24:1).

> The *first day of the week* cometh Mary Magdalene *early,* when it was yet dark, unto the sepulchre, and seeth the stone taken away from the sepulchre (John 20:1).

You see, then, that if we take literally the three days and three nights of Jonah and apply them to the length of time our Lord's body remained in the tomb, we would have to drop the idea of a Good Friday. It would appear more likely that Christ died and was buried on Wednesday afternoon, was resurrected on Saturday evening, and therefore remained in the tomb three whole days and nights, approximately seventy-two hours.

The skeptic might ask, "How did Jonah know that he had spent that much time in the belly of the fish?" We don't know. Possibly he was told afterward by the sailors. There are difficulties and obscure passages in the Scriptures, but our attitude toward the Bible as a whole is what will determine our reactions toward the difficulties in any particular section of the Bible.

The story is told of a minister who, while on a train, sat opposite an atheist. They were in the dining car preparing to eat when the unbeliever struck up a conversation. The atheist, when he found out that his companion was a preacher of the Gospel, said, "I take it then that you believe the Bible?" To this the minister replied that he accepted the Bible as God's Holy Word. Immediately the atheist asked, "But don't you encounter things in the Bible you can't understand?"

The minister answered, "Yes, I find some things in the Bible which are hard for me to understand."

This admission emboldened the atheist and, with an air of triumph, thinking he had backed the preacher into a corner, he said, "Well, what do you do then?"

The minister happened to be eating a delicious shad which was quite bony. He looked up from his luncheon plate and said to the atheist, "I do, sir, just as I do when eating this fish. When I come to the bones, I put them to one side and go on enjoying my lunch."

B. *Jonah's Prayer* (2:1-9)

Then Jonah prayed unto the LORD his God out of the fish's belly, and said, I cried by reason of mine affliction unto the LORD, and he heard me; out of the belly of hell cried I, and thou heardest my voice. For thou hadst cast me into the deep, in the midst of the seas; and the floods compassed me about: all thy billows and thy waves passed over me. Then I said, I am cast out of thy sight; yet I will look again toward thy holy temple. The waters compassed me about, even to the soul: the depth closed me round about, the weeds were wrapped about my head. I went down to the bottoms of the mountains; the earth with her bars was about me for ever: yet hast thou brought up my life from corruption, O LORD my God.

When my soul fainted within me I remembered
the Lord: and my prayer came in unto thee, into
thine holy temple. They that observe lying vanities forsake their own mercy. But I will sacrifice
unto thee with the voice of thanksgiving; I will
pay that that I have vowed. Salvation is of the
Lord.

At first in despair and fearful of death, Jonah
soon realized that God had ·spared and preserved
him. He was then thankful that he was still alive,
and what is recorded in this chapter is an expression of thanksgiving and praise for his deliverance
from death.

One of the unfortunate things about the King
James Version of the Bible is the fact that four
different words are all translated "hell."

1. *Gehenna.* This word is derived from a Hebrew word which was used to designate a deep narrow valley south of Jerusalem called the Valley of
Hinnom. At one time it was like a city dump, only
worse. Not only trash and refuse and filth burned
there, but also the carcasses of animals and the bodies of criminals. Thus Gehenna became symbolic
of the final abode of the unrighteous. No one is
there now, for it is reserved for the future punishment of the wicked. It is used in the following
scriptures: Matthew 5:22, 29-30; 10:28; 18:9; 23:

15, 33; Mark 9:43, 45, 47; Luke 12:5, and James 3:6.

2. *Tartarus*. This word is used only once, in II Peter 2:4. It is the present dwelling place of those angels who rebelled against God and were cast out of heaven. Jude 6 mentions them. These fallen angels will be kept or reserved until the final judgment.

3. *Hades*. This word means, literally, "invisible" or "unseen." It refers to that unseen place to which the spirits of the deceased went. The Bible divides Hades (so did the pagan Greeks). The part for the righteous dead was called Paradise or Abraham's bosom. The part for the wicked dead was simply called hell.

This division existed until the death and resurrection of Jesus Christ. After He arose from the dead He emptied Hades of all believers and took them to heaven. Before this, the only men who were in heaven were Enoch, Elijah, and possibly Moses. Christ lead captivity captive, and so today when a Christian dies, he goes immediately to be with the Lord in heaven. The word *Hades* occurs in the following scriptures: Matthew 11:23; 16:18; Luke 10:15; 16:23; Acts 2:27, 31; I Corinthians 15:55; Revelation 1:18; 6:8; 20:13.

4. *Sheol*. This is the Hebrew word which is used often in the Old Testament and is usually trans-

lated "hell." It is also translated "pit" or "grave."
The context helps to determine the best translation. Its etymology is uncertain. It may have come
from a verb meaning "to ask" or "to inquire." If
so, then *Sheol* would refer to a place of inquiry,
a place where departed spirits were conjured up by
necromancers, spiritualists, and seance leaders. But
then again, *Sheol* may have been derived from a
root word meaning "a hollow place." Whatever
the etymology, *Sheol* means underworld, or nether-
world and is equivalent to *Hades* in the New Testament. In fact, the Septuagint, or Greek Old Testament, uses the word *Hades* in Jonah 2:2.

The word *affliction* (2:2) comes from a verb
meaning "to bind, tie up, restrict, or cramp." Actually, the two phrases, "my affliction" and "belly
of hell," are parallel expressions. By using them
Jonah indicated the danger he was in, the peril of
death. We see then that when Jonah cried out for
help, he cried out of the anguish of threatened
death; he thought himself cut off from God. This
was the utmost extremity for Jonah, and God
stepped in; He heard Jonah's prayer and answered.
How often must men go the last mile and come to
a dead end, so that in the moment of deepest despair God may move in! Certainly man's extremity is God's opportunity!

At first glance it seems strange that Jonah asserted that *God* had cast him into the deep sea (2:3). You recall that Jonah had commanded the ship's crew to hurl him overboard. But now Jonah's mind is fixed upon the Lord, and he knows that all that had transpired had been directed by the hand of God. This is why he spoke of the breakers and rollers as "thy billows," "thy waves." The surrounding floods or currents and the overflowing waves and billows were the servants of God. The Hebrews spoke of the deep, the water, floods, billows, and waves to express grievous distress, danger, peril, or misfortune. This is readily observed in the Psalms (cf. 42:7; 69:15).

The words spoken by Jonah in verse 4 are very similar to Psalm 31:22 in thought: "For I said in my haste, I am cut off from before thine eyes: nevertheless thou heardest the voice of my supplications when I cried unto thee." In his anguish Jonah had felt driven out from God's sight, literally tossed beyond God's eyes. Like David, Jonah too had spoken in haste and had thought himself alienated from God. But, after a moment of reflection and perhaps an inner struggle—Jonah overcame his despondency and in faith cried out that he would look again toward God's holy temple, the place where the presence of Jehovah dwelt.

Sometimes when we become depressed by trying circumstances and serious straits we ought to re-

member that the Holy Spirit lives within us. The
Spirit would speak to us and remind us that our
Lord once said, "Lo, I am with you alway, even
unto the end of the age." And again we also read
"I will never leave thee, nor forsake thee" (Heb.
13:8).

Jonah continued to express his troubled thoughts
(v. 5) and when the waters of the ocean engulfed
him, he felt deep distress and peril to his very life.
The weeds are the reeds, or sea grass, at the bottom
of the ocean. The fact that they clung about Jonah's head again indicated his helplessness and the
peril of his plight. A gruesome turban indeed!

In verse 6 the word translated "bottoms" is more
properly "the cuttings." It comes from a verb
meaning "to cut off" or "to shear." Thus, the
bottoms signify the extreme ends or extremities.
In Hebrew thought, the mountains were the foun-
dations of the earth, and the ends or bottoms extended to the subterranean ocean. As the psalmist
said, the Lord founded the earth "upon the seas,
and established it upon the floods." The word
translated "bars" is derived from a verb meaning
"to go through" or "to flee." The word is used literally when reference is made to the bars of the city
gate, as, for example, in the story of Samson at
Gaza. But here the use is figurative. Just as Job
(38:10) spoke of the sea having doors and bars,

so Jonah referred to the bars of the earth. Both the sea and the earth have their bounds, and one is not to encroach upon the other. Jonah thought of the earth beneath the waters as a walled city with its gate shut and locked with a bar, preventing him from ever again entering. From all outward appearances, and as far as he could determine, he would never again see the earth.

Jonah felt himself close to death, and the soul faintness of which he spoke (v. 7) signified great distress and despair. It is at this point in Jonah's prayer that a break is noticed—a turning point in his awful experience—for it is here that Jonah remembered God and turned to Him in prayer. There was hope in prayer, and he directed his prayer to the holy temple of Jerusalem, the place where the presence of God dwelt. It was at this time that his distress and despair disappeared.

How wonderful it is to have prayers reach the ear and heart of God! How marvelous that, through the blood shed by Jesus Christ, we have access to God the Father! Christians ought never hesitate to speak with God; indeed, they are commanded to "come boldly unto the throne of grace," to "obtain mercy, and find grace to help in time of need."

According to the Scriptures mankind is without excuse. God has revealed Himself in nature, in man's conscience and experience, in history, in

Christ, and in the Bible. And men have rejected the witness. Sin has so blinded men that they cannot see the merciful overtures of a beneficent God. In the beginning of man's history men knew God. But in failing to glorify and thank God they took their first step away from Him. Consequently a chain of reactions occurred, and men became vain in their reasonings.

When men refused the true God they started to entertain foolish, corrupt, perverse, and wicked thoughts about God; and with evil ingenuity invented a multitude of idols. They exchanged the incorruptible for the corruptible, the Creator for the creature, God for gods made in the form of man, birds, animals, and creeping things.

The awful truth taught in the first chapter of Romans is that once a man gives up God, he is subject to being given up by God. And from such a state of divine disapproval and reprobation a host of evils may flow. In other words, men who are idolaters are capable of committing very conceivable wickedness under the sun. Hence in Romans 1 the inspired writer gives a long list of debasing practices which spring from idolatry.

Now the prophet Jonah designated these gods or idols worshiped by the heathen as "lying vanities" (v. 8). The word translated "lying" means, literally, "a vapor" or "a breath." Figuratively, it means that which is worthless, empty, unsubstantial, or evanescent. It is sometimes translated "vanity," as in the book of Ecclesiastes where the writer spoke of the fruitlessness and emptiness of all human enterprise and endeavor apart from God.

The word translated "vanities" is similar to the word translated "lying." It also indicates emptiness, nothingness, and that which is lying, vain, useless, false, and deceitful.

The Hebrews commonly spoke of the gods and idols of other nations and peoples as vain things. In Isaiah 44:14-20 the prophet mocked the makers of idols and ridiculed their method of manufacture. The irrationality of the practice of idolatry was further amplified by the Apostle Paul in the book of Acts (17:22-29). If a man has a mind with which to think, ears to hear, eyes to see, and a mouth with which to speak, is he not foolish to make an idol which can do none of these things, and yet claim that idol to be a god? Is not the real Creator greater than the creature?

The word *observe* means in the original language "to guard," "to watch" or "to keep," and the force of the verb is such that it signifies a diligent reverence of these false gods—making them the object of one's trust.

We doubt if Jonah especially had in mind here the heathen sailors. He had no cause to speak contemptuously of them in particular. The crewmen had given Jonah every consideration, and even though they were heathen idolaters, this verse (v. 8) should not be construed as a direct reference to them. The expression used was typical of the Jewish attitude to all idols, and Jonah's reference to the nothingness of dead idols was calculated to heighten his praise of the living God!

The God of Israel, Jonah's God, was and is the only true source of mercy, goodness, and kindness—that loving-kindness which condescends to the needs of God's creatures. In Him alone is there true salvation and deliverance. Jonah's point was that when men serve idols they abandon their only source of succor. They forsake or cut off themselves from Him who alone is able to help.

Perhaps some say to all this, "So what? What contemporary relevance has all this talk about idolatry? We are civilized people, not heathen bowing and scraping before statues and images." Yes, we are civilized. But we are also idolaters! Not in the crude way of Jonah's time, but in a more subtle, sophisticated, and therefore sinister way. We have merely made some substitutions: in the place of Ashtaroth, Baal, Chemosh, Dagon, Diana, Isis, Mammon, Molech, and Nebo we have put alcohol, ambition, automobiles, greed, Hollywood, jazz, money, nicotine, pleasure, science, sports, and sex.

Moreover, many in "Christian" America classify themselves as Buddhists, Muslims, or adherents of some other religion. Hundreds of millions in other lands still worship heathen gods.

In contrast to the heathen, whose worship was vain and empty, Jonah was determined not to go empty-handed before the true God (v. 9). Idolaters may forget and forsake the true source of mercy, but Jonah would not. He promised to give God thanks and to praise Him in song. Jonah's vow was not extraordinary or peculiar; it was common for Jews to make vows in time of need, with the expectation of keeping the promise after relief was granted.

The Hebrew word for "salvation" has given us the name Joshua, and its Greek rendering, Jesus. Joshua is a contraction of *Jehoshua,* which means "Jehovah is salvation." God often used men to bring about deliverance so that salvation through human instrumentality does not contradict Jonah's statement. Whatever deliverance was effected, God was the power behind it. Jonah now knew by experience that the help he needed could come only from the Lord.

The salvation of which Jonah spoke was primarily one of deliverance from physical difficulties and dangers. However, the Hebrew word used is not necessarily confined to external evils. The mode and extent of the salvation is not limited. It may be used of national salvation, for example, as in Israel's deliverance from Egypt. (See Exodus 14: 30, where we find the first occurrence of the word *saved*.) It also depicts the deliverance of individuals—the poor, the humble, the contrite, the needy, the meek, the righteous.

Furthermore, this word involves not only physical deliverance but salvation and preservation from moral troubles. In other words, in God man will find deliverance from every kind of spiritual and temporal evil. The same thing can be said of the Greek New Testament word which is translated "salvation." It too may be used of both a temporal and a spiritual deliverance, although in the New Testament the spiritual sense predominates. It is accurate and biblical to say of the spiritual sense: "I have been saved, I am being saved, and I shall be saved."

To say, "I have been saved," is to speak of justification, or of a good and right relationship with God. When a man believes in the blood of Jesus Christ he is put in good standing with God; there is no longer enmity between God and that man. Thus, to speak of salvation as an accomplished fact means that the penalty of sin, which is spiritual death, has been paid by the Lord Jesus Christ. And the man who believes in Christ stands justified in

God's sight. The following scriptures in the King James Version were found to have either an aorist or perfect tense in the original Greek and therefore indicate an accomplished fact: Romans 8:24; Ephesians 2:5, 8; and II Timothy 1:9.

The present tense of salvation enables the saint to say, "I am being saved." In the process of being saved, which is sometimes called sanctification, the daily battle over the power of sin is fought and, by the power of the risen Christ, the saint is enabled to live victoriously. The present phase of the word "salvation" is not too clearly seen in our King James Version. However, the present tense of the Greek verb is used in I Corinthians 1:18; 15:2; and II Corinthians 2:15.

The third aspect of salvation is observed in the use of the future tense, as in Romans 8:24. This phase of salvation is sometimes called glorification, which has to do with the body. As long as we are in our physical body, sin will be present in us. The old nature remains in us. But when the Lord Jesus Christ comes back, the bodies of all saints— whether dead or alive—will be changed. It is at this time that we will know in a better way the full and complete meaning of salvation. Certainly Jonah's knowledge was incomplete, but he knew enough to say, "Salvation is of the Lord."

C. *God's Direction* (2:10)

And the LORD spake unto the fish, and it vomited
out Jonah upon the dry land.

Indeed, deliverance was of God. The Lord who
had commanded the ravens to feed the prophet
Elijah now spoke to the fish, and the creature
which had swallowed Jonah and kept him alive
three days and three nights now vomited him out
upon the dry land.

This verb meaning "to vomit up," "to spue out,"
or "to disgorge" is usually associated with evil
events. For example, Jehovah threatened the Israelites with expulsion from the land if they were un-
faithful and disobedient to Him. They were
warned that the land would spue them out (Lev.
18:25, 28). In the book of Revelation the self-sat-
isfied, lukewarm church of Laodicea was warned
of being spued out of God's mouth (3:16).

The wicked man who is rich with unjust gain
will vomit it up again (Job 20:15). Even as too
much honey can nauseate (Prov. 25:16), so can
the sweet flattering words of an evil man (Prov.
23:8). The fool who loves his sin and returns to
his foolishness is compared with a dog who returns
to his own vomit (Prov. 26:11; II Peter 2:22).

Finally, most of the vomiting spoken of in the
Bible deals with drunkenness: Isaiah 19:14; 28:8;

Jeremiah 25:27; 48:26 (the drunkenness of pride). Is it not peculiar that the alcohol and beer industries always portray their customers as cheerful, smiling people having a good time?

But such advertising is good business; you can imagine what would happen if their advertisements depicted the automobile accidents, broken homes, wrecked marriages, immorality, empty pocketbooks, red eyes, wounds without cause (Prov. 23:29), the vomit on the streets, and other results of drinking. Then, of course, their products might not sell so readily.

It appears then that Jonah's deliverance is the only pleasant use of the word *vomit* in the Bible. Exactly where Jonah was cast forth (Septuagint) is not known, but it is most likely that he landed upon the coast of Palestine near the city of Joppa.

PART II

The Second Commission

Chapter 1

COMMISSION RENEWED
(3:1-2)

And the word of the LORD came unto Jonah the second time, saying, Arise, go unto Nineveh, that great city, and preach unto it the preaching that I bid thee.

Now the very fact that the Lord spoke again to Jonah is quite revealing. First of all, the command manifested Jehovah's continued love and concern for the heathen Ninevites. He had no intention of abandoning this great city simply because of one prophet's disobedience and waywardness.

Second, the order demonstrated God's mercy to Jonah. The horrifying experience in the belly of the fish had taught Jonah at least one lesson and, judging by his prayer, he had learned it well. Forgiven, he now received a second chance to warn the Ninevites to flee the wrath of God which was to come.

We are moved to speak of Jonah's God as the God of the Second Chance. But honest sober reflection compels the saint to speak of Him as the God of the 999th chance! Such gracious mercy as was extended to Jonah here, and to David, and to the thief dying upon the cross, and to Peter—surely it has been granted to all believers through the precious blood of Jesus Christ.

What genuine Christian dares to count the number of times God has forgiven his conscious and presumptuous sins, has removed the otherwise inevitable consequences of those sins, and has restored fellowship? How many times has forgiveness been asked and granted, and another opportunity given to make good for Christ! How marvelous is the forebearance and patience and mercy of God!

When the Lord first spoke to Jonah the command was to arise, to go, and to cry against Nineveh. The prophet was told that Nineveh's wickedness had ascended before God. The second command was the same: arise, go, and preach (the same Hebrew word translated "cry" in 1:2). However, the wickedness of Nineveh is not mentioned this time.

Jonah's prayer while in the fish had been heard, and the Lord had forgiven him, so the reiteration of the command was not a reproach for his disobedience. This time God emphasizes the content of Jonah's preaching. He is told to preach only that which God bade him. This is still good advice for all preachers: preach only that which God commands. We live in an age in which society tends to dictate to the preacher, and social pressures and modern theological trends seek to obscure the fact that God calls men into the ministry, equips them, and bids them preach His Word.

The exact content of Jonah's preaching is not disclosed here, although in verse 4 the basic message is given. It is important to note that Jonah was not to speak of himself. In the New Testament the Apostle Peter wrote: "If any man speak, let him speak as the oracles of God" (I Peter 4:11), and John the Baptist said, "He whom God hath sent speaketh the words of God" (John 3:34). Obedience to God's Word was stressed also in the preaching ministries of Moses, Jeremiah, and the disciples, and in the ministry of every prophet who said, "Thus saith the Lord."

It was predicted by the Apostle Paul that the time would come when people would dictate to the minister what they wanted to hear. The time would come, he said, when men would not endure sound solid instruction, but after their own desires would collect teachers and preachers who would tickle their itching ears. Ministers of the Gospel need to hear anew the voice of God saying to them, "Preach the preaching that I bid thee!"

CHAPTER 2

OBEDIENCE
(3:3-4)

So Jonah arose, and went unto Nineveh, according to the word of the LORD. Now Nineveh was an exceeding great city of three days' journey. And Jonah began to enter into the city a day's journey, and he cried, and said, Yet forty days, and Nineveh shall be overthrown.

This time there was no attempt to avoid and disobey the will of God. There was no hesitation nor show of reluctance. Having heard the command, Jonah arose and went to the city. Note how often the greatness of Nineveh is mentioned (1:2; 3:2-3; 4:11). Some scholars, because the findings of archaeologists have not yet corroborated the Biblical description of Nineveh as such an extensive city, have termed this description either an inaccuracy or an exaggeration. Some have suggested it is just a poetic expression or a magnified afterthought. Still others have suggested that this "exceeding great city" was a complex of cities comparable to Greater Philadelphia, which term includes several neighboring cities and towns.

Strange as it may seem, some commentators emphasize the word *was*. They claim that the book of Jonah was written after the city of Nineveh had been destroyed. In other words, Nineveh had ceased to be a great city, and did not even exist during the time of Jonah's ministry or by the time the book was written. Let us consider another verse in the same way: "Now Bethany *was* nigh unto Jerusalem, about fifteen furlongs off . . ." (John 11:18). Who would stress the verb *was* to the point of suggesting that the town of Bethany did not exist in Jesus' time, or even when Luke wrote? Certainly the context will not support such a rendering.

Such suggestions are unlikely and unnecessary. Arguments based upon lack of archaeological evidence are not very sound arguments. Furthermore, nothing found thus far in Biblical lands has ever contradicted the historical truths of the Bible. And nothing ever will! If the Lord desires that something be discovered which will further attest the historical accuracy of the book of Jonah, then we will rejoice and praise Him. But in the meantime we take God at His word. Nineveh was a *great* city!

Now the three days referred to are usually interpreted to mean the amount of time it would have taken to walk around the city. But the three days journey may refer to the time it would take to walk through the city. What is true of cities now was true then; namely, each town had some main thoroughfare or principal street. And since the word translated "journey" means "walk," the perfectly natural implication is that it would take three days to walk through Nineveh from one end of its main street to the other end.

Of course the prophet must have stopped frequently along the way, visiting principal places and preaching to the inhabitants. In this way a considerable proportion of the population would have been reached with his message of impending doom.

Finally, an understanding of the Hebraic concept involved here will throw more light upon the city of Nineveh. The Hebrew text says literally: "Now Nineveh was a city—great to [before] God, a journey of three days." When a thing is put in relationship with God, some characteristic of that object is heightened, magnified, or increased. This Hebraism or Hebrew mode of expression is seen also in the following scriptures:

Genesis 23:6: ". . . thou art a mighty prince among us." This is, literally, in the Hebrew, "prince of God."

Genesis 30:8: ". . . with great wrestlings have I wrestled . . ." This is in the Hebrew, literally "wrestlings of God."

Psalm 36:6: "Thy righteousness is like the great mountains; . . ." Literally, this is "the mountains of God."

Psalm 80:10: ". . . the boughs thereof were like the goodly cedars." Literally, this is the "cedars of God."

This Hebrew way of speaking is found also in the New Testament book of Acts: "In which time Moses was born, and was exceeding fair" (7:20). The Greek is literally, "fair to God." It is evident that in the Hebrew mind the quality of a thing is increased when that thing is closely related to God. Whatever adjective is used to describe a thing, the quality of it is raised to a higher degree if it is connected with God. It shows that God was not impressed by the size or fame of the city of Nineveh. But the many lost souls of Nineveh were of great concern to God and the task of moving to repentance a pagan metropolis steeped in sin was a herculean task indeed. So when God called Nineveh "that great city," Jonah would be impressed with the magnitude of the task before him.

The expression translated "he began to enter" has been interpreted in various ways. Some believe that the moment Jonah set foot in the city he started to preach. Others claim that he first completed a day's journey into the city and at the end of that first day started to preach. However, we would suggest that Jonah entered the city, and then, somewhere along the way during this first day's journey, began to preach his message of judgment.

There was nothing hidden or apocryphal about Jonah's message, nor was it flowery and oratorical. His message was simple and direct. He spoke Aramaic, a language known to both Hebrew and Assyrian alike (cf. Isa. 36:11). It seems ridiculous for some scholars to assume that Jonah was not historical simply because they have no evidence that Jonah could speak a language that the Ninevites understood.

"Forty days, and Nineveh shall be overthrown!" Probably this was not all that Jonah said, but it was the main thrust of his message. He stressed the impending doom, and the simplicity of his message was impressive. In the Septuagint, and according to the Arabic, it was three days and not forty.

However, since the number forty is considered the number of probation, testing, punishment, chastisement, and humiliation, we accept the reading "forty days." For example, the rain fell upon the earth for forty days and nights and caused the great Flood. Moses spent his first forty years in Egypt, the next forty in Midian, and his last forty with Israel, wandering in the desert wilderness. He spent forty days and nights upon Mt. Sinai with the Lord. The prophet Elijah went forty days and nights unto Mt. Horeb in the strength of the food that God provided under the juniper tree. Finally, there is the temptation of the Lord Jesus in the wilderness for forty days and nights.

The verb translated "shall be overthrown" means literally to turn or overturn. The tense of the verb indicates thoroughness—a complete destruction or overturning of the city's foundation is meant. The manner in which this was to be done is not disclosed. But it is interesting to note that this same verb is used to describe the destruction of the cities of Sodom and Gomorrah. This destruction, it may be remembered, was accomplished by brimstone and fire from the Lord out of heaven.

Things are so fixed in nature, conscience, and history that man has absolutely no excuse for continued disobedience. The warnings of judgment are evidence of God's mercy, for He is not willing that any should perish. He never has sprung surprises upon mankind, but has always given warning of judgment. There is the story of an old Greek philosopher who upon one occasion was given a severe tongue lashing by his wife. He listened to her in silence, and his silence infuriated her the more. Finally, she took a bucket of cold water and threw it upon him. Though soaking wet from head to foot, he remarked very calmly, and somewhat philosophically, "After that thunder and lightning storm, I rather expected a shower."

Just as the old philosopher was not surprised by his wife's actions, neither should man be surprised by God's judgmental actions. From the very beginning of history the Lord has warned of judgment. In the Garden of Eden, Adam was commanded not to eat of the tree of the knowledge of good and evil. God warned him, "In the day that thou eatest thereof thou shalt surely die."

Noah preached righteousness and warned the people of the coming flood. But when the time of judgment came, multitudes perished. Though God had warned, only eight souls were saved. On another occasion, God revealed to Abraham the plan to destroy Sodom and Gomorrah. Abraham's nephew, Lot, who lived in Sodom, was a witness against the perverted men of Sodom and also warned his own sons-in-law to flee from Sodom. Despite the warnings of impending doom, they laughed in Lot's face.

To Joseph was revealed the interpretations of
the dreams of Pharaoh and, hearkening to the voice
of God, Egypt survived the seven years of leanness
and famine. The dreams of Pharaoh were the
warnings of God. Moses and Aaron stood before
the Pharaoh of Egypt and warned him of the consequence of failing to let Israel go. Indignant,
Pharaoh inquired, "Who is the Lord, that I should
obey his voice to let Israel go?" The ten plagues
were the result of such arrogance. Elijah the prophet prophesied against Ahab and warned him of the
coming drought. Belshazzar was drinking wine
from the vessels which had been taken from the
temple in Jerusalem when he saw the handwriting
on the wall—the warning of God.

Stephen rehearsed the mercies and warnings of
God toward Israel and showed the members of the
Sanhedrin how Israel had despised God's grace and
resisted the Holy Ghost. At Mars Hill, Paul the
apostle also spoke of God's mercy in dealing with
man's ignorance. Judgment was sure to come, he
said, and the assurance of it was the resurrection
of Christ. The resurrection of the Lord Jesus Christ
was the guarantee of a coming judgment. The
Athenians mocked, and put the matter off.

So against the background of these examples of
warning, we view the ministry of the prophet Jonah, whose prediction of doom was in itself an act

of mercy. Men everywhere and in all ages ought not to despise the riches of God's goodness, His forbearance, and long-suffering.

CHAPTER 3

CONSEQUENCE OF OBEDIENCE
(3:5-10)

A. *Repentance* (3:5-9)

So the people of Nineveh believed God, and proclaimed a fast, and put on sackcloth, from the greatest of them even to the least of them. For word came unto the king of Nineveh, and he arose from his throne, and he laid his robe from him, and covered him with sackcloth, and sat in ashes. And he caused it to be proclaimed and published through Nineveh by the decree of the king and his nobles, saying, Let neither man nor beast, herd nor flock, taste any thing: let them not feed, nor drink water: but let man and beast be covered with sackcloth, and cry mightily unto God: yea, let them turn every one from his evil way, and from the violence that is in their hands. Who can tell if God will turn and repent, and turn away from his fierce anger, that we perish not?

When it is said that the people of Nineveh "believed God," it is meant that they acknowledged Jonah was a prophet and accepted as true what Jonah preached. The word translated "believed" comes from a verb meaning "to confirm" or "to support." The tense used gives the idea of considering as confirmed, taking as established; hence, what Jonah preached was regarded as true.

The response of the city was immediate. It was an opportune moment, for the people had heard about Jonah earlier—from the returned seamen. Now they were impressed by Jonah's appearance in their city. Jonah must have been a sign to them, for on one occasion the scribes and Pharisees requested to be shown a sign and our Lord said, "An evil and adulterous generation seeketh after a sign; and there shall no sign be given to it, but the sign of the prophet Jonas" (Matt. 12:39).

The sign referred to was the experience of Jonah —his being cast out into the ocean, delivered, and returned to dry land. The Lord added, "The men of Nineveh shall rise in judgment with this generation, and shall condemn it: because they repented at the preaching of Jonas; and, behold, a greater than Jonas is here" (Matt. 12:41).

It was the Lord's desire to impress upon the scribes and the Pharisees their own miserable condition. He accomplished this by using comparisons in which He was shown to be superior. Jonah was far inferior to the Lord Jesus. In the first place, Jonah's awful experience was the result of disobedience. Second, Jonah did not actually die, but remained alive inside the fish for three days and nights. Third, his mission was to the heathen, the unenlightened. Fourth, he did no miracles.

On the other hand, Christ willingly obeyed His Father and came to this earth. He performed many miracles as He ministered among the Jews, a religiously enlightened people. Finally, He died for the sins of all men, was buried, and then resurrected to live forevermore.

Jonah's work in Nineveh was brief and its effect short-lived. Christ's work continues—even today—all over the world. In short, Christ was the superior prophet, Jonah the inferior. And yet the Ninevites responded favorably to Jonah's ministry. The Jews believed neither the miracles, the preaching, or the resurrection of Christ. These facts, said Christ, will face them in the day of judgment.

Two outward signs of repentance were demonstrated by the Ninevites—fasting and putting on sackcloth. Fasting is defined as abstaining from food altogether, eating sparingly, or abstaining from specific foods. Hence, any restriction in diet may be considered fasting. According to the Scriptures, the following individuals fasted: Ahab, Anna,

Barnabas, Christ, Cornelius, Daniel, Darius, David, Elijah, Esther, Moses, Nehemiah, and Paul. The Israelites fasted many times, as did also the church leaders at Antioch and other cities.

A study of the scriptures reveals a variety of reasons for fasting: affliction, calamity, consternation, death, defeat, despair, grief, humility, invasion, prayer power, repentance, sorrow, testing, trials, tribulation, worship, and so on. Fasting certainly has some value, even though there is no New Testament command for Christians to fast. From a physical viewpoint it might be beneficial for many of us to cut down our food intake, and thereby lose excess weight.

You may recall also that on one occasion the disciples were told that fasting (and prayer) was a necessary ingredient for the increased spiritual power they needed to cast out demons. However, we could take the fasting here in a spiritual sense, meaning self-denial in general.

According to the psalmist, fasting may serve to humble and chasten the soul, and in this way prove a blessing. Of course, there is always the danger of the fast becoming an act of hypocrisy and pride. God repeatedly warned Israel of this. The New Testament saint must be sure he is led by the Holy Spirit in this matter of fasting.

The second external sign of repentance was the

wearing of sackcloth. Sackcloth was a coarse, rough, dark-colored cloth usually made of goat hair or camel hair, or even of flax, hemp, or cotton. It was used for making sacks for grain and also for clothing. When worn as a garment it was a sign of mourning, distress, humiliation, penitence, or protest.

And so it was that everybody was influenced by Jonah's message. The young and old, the famous and the insignificant—all believed God, and demonstrated their repentance with the outward signs of fasting and wearing of sackcloth.

Some scholars have been unable to accept the words "king of Nineveh" (v. 6) and have decided that the book of Jonah is fiction. They claim that if the story of Jonah was a true story the king would have been called the king of Assyria and not the king of Nineveh, and his proper name would have been given.

But once again the argument from silence fails. In the absence of Assyrian parallels or any definite information, we have really scant basis for denying the historical accuracy of the book. The writer may have used the Semitic word *mlk* (*melek* in Hebrew, meaning "king") in its Akkadian sense, where *malku* means "prince," "governor." The word "decree" in 3:7 is an Aramaism following the Akkadian meaning of *ta'am*, "royal edict," whereas the ordinary Hebrew meaning elsewhere is "taste," "discretion." Thus we do have Akkadianisms here. Any man with the proper concept of the origin of the Scriptures will never be willing to deny the veracity and historical accuracy of the Bible. The writer of the book of Hebrews said, "Without faith it is impossible to please him: for he that cometh to God must believe that he is, and that he is a rewarder of them that diligently seek him" (Heb. 11:6).

The Christian approaches the Scriptures in the same way. He comes to the Bible believing that it is the Word of God. This is the only attitude which is Christ-honoring; it is the only viewpoint of Scripture which will be a blessing to the Bible student, and for which he will be rewarded.

When the news reached the king, he got up from his throne, put off his cloak, and humbled himself by putting on sackcloth and ashes. Once again some scholars have rearranged verses in this chapter in order to make it appear that the king acted before the people of the city did. However, this is not necessary. It would be highly unnatural to assume that the people who first heard Jonah remained unmoved and unrepentant until the king himself took some action. The repentance which came was not the result of the king's orders but rather the outcome of the preaching of Jonah, the servant of the true God.

Unlike Moses before Pharaoh, Jonah had not demanded an audience before the king. No! Jonah began preaching in the streets of the city the first day of his mission.

We noted earlier two outward signs of repentance—fasting and the wearing of sackcloth. Now, here is a third—the use of ashes. The word *ashes* first occurs in Genesis 18:27. Abraham, interceding for the cities of Sodom and Gomorrah, said, "Behold now, I have taken upon me to speak unto the Lord, which am but dust and ashes." Abraham thus spoke figuratively of his own insignificance. Elsewhere in the Scriptures ashes upon the head signified humiliation; for example, in the case of Tamar who was defiled by Ammon (II Sam. 13: 19).

The use of ashes signified contrition when Daniel prayed for his people and when Job admitted the greatness of the Lord. For Mordecai and the Jews, and for Job in affliction, it was a sign of grief and mourning. Figuratively it depicted the ignominy and defeat to which the devil and the wicked will be brought. In Isaiah 44:20 the expression "he feedeth on ashes" conveyed the thought of worthlessness. And, finally, ashes speak figuratively of sorrow and distress.

When the news came, the king called his council together, and prepared an official edict telling the people to do that which they had already begun to do. The king made a proclamation which was published throughout the city.

Note in verse 7 the words *decree* and *taste*. Both are derived from the same verb. "To taste" means here "to eat in a small quantity." Once a thing is tasted, some judgment may be made, some decision arrived at, something discerned or perceived. The decision, judgment, or decree then is the result of having perceived or tasted something.

Notice also that the animals were included. The beasts mentioned were the beasts of burden, such as the horses and mules. The herd included the cattle and oxen, and the flock meant the sheep and goats. The word translated "feed" means "to pasture" or "to graze," and supports the fact that the writer had in mind the animals just mentioned. These were animals good for food or service—or both—and, of course, were tame or domesticated.

Why were these animals involved? To show total repentance. The beasts were property and, as such, were considered a part of the person who owned them. Furthermore, animals live with men and are affected by the deeds of men. Someone has called it "biotic rapport." This relationship of brute creation with man is taught in the Bible, and we can see it in our own experiences. Before the Fall, Adam lived in perfect peace and harmony with the creatures in the Garden of Eden. After the Fall, man's relationship with animals was altered; today wild beasts cannot be trusted.

Only when the Lord Jesus Christ sets up His earthly kingdom will there be such peace as existed in the Garden of Eden. "The wolf also shall dwell with the lamb, and the leopard shall lie down with the kid; and the calf and the young lion and the fatling together; and a little child shall lead them. And the cow and the bear shall feed; their young ones shall lie down together: and the lion shall eat straw like the ox. And the sucking child shall play on the hole of the viper, and the weaned child shall put his hand on the adder's den" (Isa. 11:6-8, ASV).

In Romans 8:19-23 we are taught that all creation was affected by sin, and groans painfully even now in anticipation of the day when God will reveal His sons along with Christ and deliver the creation from the bondage of corruption. So we see that there is a relationship between man and beast. And the Ninevites believed that afflicting the animals would help impress God with their repentance. The cry of the beast would be heard by God and add to the total picture of their mourning.

The fact that the Lord does hear the animals is amply taught in Scripture.

> Who provideth for the raven his prey, when his young ones cry unto God, and wander for lack of food (Job 38:41, ASV)?

> How do the beasts groan! the herds of cattle are perplexed, because they have no pasture; yea, the flocks of sheep are made desolate. . . . The beasts of the field cry also unto thee: for the rivers of waters are dried up, and the fire hath devoured the pastures of the wilderness (Joel 1:18, 20).

It is evident that withholding food and water from the animals would cause them to groan and cry out to God. It was the belief of the Ninevites that extending the external signs of repentance and sorrow in this manner would demonstrate to God their intense determination to cease their iniquity.

The king's order to put sackcloth on the animals is mentioned in verse 8, and showed how intense was the king's desire for total repentance. The decree ordered the people not only to show the outward signs of repentance such as fasting, wearing of sackcloth, and crying aloud, but also to take some moral action. Everyone was ordered to turn from, or forsake, his evil way. The word *way* is used figuratively, meaning the course of life or action or undertaking. Each man was to turn away from his wicked actions—his evil behavior.

And then, in parallel exhortation, each man was
ordered to turn from the violence which was in his
hands. The word translated "violence" also means
wrong—either physical or ethical wrong, or both.
According to sacred and secular history, Assyria's
chief sin was her cruelty. And, of course, what was
true of Assyria as a nation also characterized indi-
vidual Ninevites.

The violence referred to in this verse refers spe-
cifically to physical violence, but it may include
also injurious language, harsh treatment, and—in
general—man's rude wickedness and his noisy, wild
ruthlessness. The hands obviously represent the
instruments with which the violence was com-
mitted—the tools with which the violence was done.
Job denied that there was any injustice in his hands
(Job 16:17). David spake of the cleanness of his
hands (Ps. 18:20); and Isaiah once informed Israel
that one cause of their calamity was the "act of violence in their hands" (Isa. 59:6).

"Who can tell" (v. 9) means "who knows."
These words are not a question of doubt or uncertainty so much as they are an expression of hope.
Nothing in Jonah's message suggested God's par-
don, but the very fact that Nineveh was warned
must be considered an act of mercy.

We see here the value of judgment preaching.
Some people are dismayed by "hellfire and brim-

stone" preaching, and claim that it does great harm. They say that it is medieval and that it creates fear and feelings of guilt. It is true that fear and a guilt complex may be the product of judgment preaching, but who is to say whether this is all bad? It may well be beneficial. To be forewarned can lead to being forearmed. Certainly Jonah's preaching of approaching doom led the king and the nobles to express the hope of averting the consequences of the burning anger of Jonah's God.

Two Hebrew words are translated "repent." One word means "to turn back" or "to return." The second word is the one found in the verse we are considering (v. 9), and it means "to be sorry" or "to console oneself."

The Bible speaks of human repentance and of divine repentance. We know from daily practical experience that human repentance may be either true or false. Callous and unthinking men may be sorry about the result of sin but feel no remorse because of the sin itself. They are only sorry they were caught.

We are reminded of the story of the young hoodlum in Chicago who murdered a policeman in a tavern on the south side. Before midnight he was caught and put in jail. The next day his noon meal was served to him, and when he saw what was on the plate he yelled out, "What's this?" The orderly replied, "It's mutton." Then the thug yelled back, "Take it away! Do you think I would eat meat on Friday?"

This story points out that there may be conformity or adherence to a religious system or ritual but no true inward change of heart. The man under treatment for gonorrhea may temporarily forgo fulfilling his sexual lust; the alcoholic may be frightened by the doctor and temporarily abandon the whiskey bottle; the nicotine fiend may give up temporarily his addiction to cigarettes after reading scientific surveys about lung cancer. And so it goes —there may be temporary external changes but no permanent internal change at all!

Certainly the Scriptures teach that the citizens of Nineveh repented. And we accept the record. We have no other historical records making mention of it, but to argue that no such revival ever occurred is really not reasonable. It has been stated earlier, and we repeat it now: the argument from silence is unreliable. It may well have been the habit of the Assyrians to ignore recording such things. The few Assyrian records extant make no mention of religious revivals or military defeats, but refer only to their political achievements and military victories.

It would appear that the revival was not long lasting. It was superficial, shallow, and short-lived;

there was no deep moral reform, no change of heart, mind, or disposition produced by God's Spirit and accompanied by sorrow arising from the sense of sin.

B. *Deliverance* (3:10)

And God saw their works, that they turned from their evil way; and God repented of the evil, that he had said that he would do unto them; and he did it not.

Although the same Hebrew word is used with respect to human repentance and divine repentance, the latter requires explanation. Often in the Old Testament record, human characteristics were ascribed to God. We call this anthropomorphism, literally, man-form. It means to describe God after the manner of men.

For example, we see with our eyes, and since we know that God sees all things, therefore we say God has eyes (Gen. 6:8; Deut. 11:12; II Chron. 16:9). Human beings make things with their hands; therefore, whatever God has wrought is ascribed to His hands (Job 12:9; Ps. 17:7). And so it goes in other scriptures where mention is made of God's back (Isa. 38:17), mouth (Deut. 8:3), finger (Exodus 31:18). Thus, that which is not human is interpreted in human characteristics. This manner of describing God is an accommodation to our finite minds in order that we might better understand the infinite.

This likewise holds true with regard to divine repentance. The Lord is not ignorant, weak, feeble, or fallible; so He should not change His mind. He knows all things and sees all things from the beginning to the end. But events may take place which appear, from man's viewpoint, to be variations in God's plans.

Take, for example, the story of Hezekiah. Isaiah came one day and said to him, "Thus saith the Lord, set thine house in order; for thou shalt die, and not live." As you recall, Hezekiah prayed and the Lord of mercy spared him to live another fifteen years. From man's viewpoint it would appear that God repented or changed His mind. But this would not be true. God does not change, for in Him there is no variableness, neither shadow of turning. The Lord knew all along what would happen in the life of Hezekiah.

Many Old Testament scriptures speak of God repenting: Genesis 6:6-7; Exodus 32:12, 14; Numbers 23:19; I Samuel 15:10-11, 29, 35; II Samuel 24:16; I Chronicles 21:15; Psalm 106:45; 110:4; Jeremiah 4:28; 18:8, 10; 20:16; 26:13, 19; 42:10; Ezekiel 24:14; Joel 2:13-14; Amos 7:3, 6, and Zechariah 8:14. And from man's viewpoint, God changed His mind about destroying the city of

Nineveh. Judgment was withheld. God has no pleasure in the death of the wicked, and we see that it was His purpose not to destroy Nineveh at this time. The Lord knew that Jonah's preaching would be heeded and that Nineveh would be spared.

Notice that the word *evil* occurs twice in verse 10. The Hebrew word is the same in both occurrences, but the connotations are different. The evil way of the Ninevites was moral wickedness and cruelty. The evil of which it is said God repented was nonmoral; it refers to distress, destruction, catastrophe, or calamity which may result from the judgment of God. This is the idea expressed in Isaiah 45:7: "I form the light, and create darkness: I make peace, and create *evil*: I the LORD do all these things."

And so God spared Nineveh.

CHAPTER 4

DISPLEASURE MANIFESTED
(4:1-11)

A. *Anger Expressed* (4:1-4)

But it displeased Jonah exceedingly, and he was very angry. And he prayed unto the LORD, and said, I pray thee, O LORD, was not this my saying, when I was yet in my country? Therefore I fled before unto Tarshish: for I knew that thou art a gracious God, and merciful, slow to anger, and of great kindness, and repentest thee of the evil. Therefore now, O LORD, take I beseech thee, my life from me; for it is better for me to die than to live. Then said the LORD, Doest thou well to be angry?

The word translated "displeased" is derived from a verb meaning "to be evil" or "to be bad." From Jonah's viewpoint the deliverance of Nineveh was evil, and it vexed and irritated him. The word *angry* comes from a verb meaning "to burn" or "to be kindled." We often hear a colloquial expression about someone who is very angry: "He is burned up." It is interesting to note that the Apostle Paul used, in a figurative sense, the verb for setting on fire or burning up to indicate being inflamed with indignation: "Who is weak, and I am not weak? Who is offended, and I burn not?" (II Cor. 11:29).

The Septuagint softens Jonah's sentiments somewhat: "And Jonah was grieved [pained, distressed] with a great grief, and was confused [confounded]." Doubtless, Jonah's feeling included disapproval, grief, and vexation, but it was stronger than these emotions. The word denotes the ardor of emotion felt by Jonah and should not be softened simply because it reflects badly upon his character. He was exceedingly angry.

The proper interpretation of verse 2 will help us to understand better the motives behind the prophet's disobedience. Earlier (1:3) no explanation was given for Jonah's actions. We simply attributed his rebellion to self-will and left the matter there. But now we see a reason for the rebellion—a reason Jonah himself offered. And this in turn affords insight into the reason for the displeasure he expressed at the deliverance of Nineveh. Jonah strongly entreated the Lord and said: "Was not this my thought? Is it not what I said to myself when I was yet in Israel? This is why I fled before-hand to Tarshish!''

The word *before* does not refer back to the time of Jonah's act of rebellion as if to say, "That's why I fled the first time!" The idea is better put: "I ran away in anticipation of your doing the very thing you have done. I fled in order to forestall it." The word *before* is derived from the verb meaning "to come" or "to be in front," and it means here "to be beforehand, anticipate, fore-stall." In Psalm 119:147-148, it is translated as "prevented," which is an old English word mean-ing "to precede" or "to go before."

The name of God in this verse is *El,* and this is the first and only time it occurs in the book of Jo-nah. Where the Hebrew word is *Yahweh,* the King James Version translated "LORD," and *Elohim* is translated "God." *Yahweh* [or Jehovah] is the most frequently used name for God in the Old Tes-tament. There is some haziness about its meaning and pronunciation. In Exodus 3:14 the expres-sion "I AM THAT I AM" includes the verb "to be," but most scholars prefer the verb "to become." Of course, there are many interpretations of the meaning of the name Yahweh or Jehovah. For ex-ample: the Self-existent One, the Eternal, the Cre-ator, Giver of Existence, Performer of His Promises, I Am Who I Am, and He Who Becomes Whatever Is Necessary.

Two things we may be certain about are the following: the name of Jehovah expresses the eternality of God, and it is very closely related to the redemption of Israel. With respect to this last matter, it might be said that no man who is not a faithful Jew can truthfully call himself a Jehovah's Witness.

The name *Elohim* is the first one encountered in the Bible (Gen. 1:1). It is a plural noun and simply means God, probably signifying strength or power. *El* is a simplified form of *Elohim* and means "the Mighty One, God who is able to carry out His will." Jonah, then, spoke of the Mighty One capable of achieving His slightest desire, as the gracious Mighty One. The word translated "gracious" is derived from a verb meaning "to show favor." God's kindness and favor, freely bestowed upon undeserving men and women by a God who is mighty, springs out of His love for man.

The second thing Jonah knew was that God was merciful. This word comes from a verb meaning "to love" and "to have compassion." It expresses the Lord's feelings when He beholds feeble man in all his weakness, helplessness, and suffering. Elsewhere it is translated "pity."

The third attribute of God which Jonah claimed to know was His quality of long-suffering. God was slow to anger. The word translated "slow" means "long (in time)." There are many Old Testament passages which point out that the Lord does not always immediately execute deserved punishment, but is long-suffering. The people of God are exhorted to be like God in this characteristic of slowness to anger.

Fourth, Jonah stated that he knew that great kindness also was characteristic of God. The word expresses God's loving-kindness in condescending to the needs of His creatures. It is often translated "mercy," and sometimes is translated "kindness, pity, favor, goodness."

Fifth, Jonah knew that God was capable of repenting of the evil or calamity intended for the ungodly. We have already discussed the meaning of divine repentance.

So we find a partial answer to the question, "Why did Jonah run away?" in Jonah's description of the attributes of God. Possibly Jonah reasoned in this way: "I am sent to warn Nineveh. These Ninevites are Gentile dogs and hate Israel and hate the God of Israel. But suppose the warning is heeded, then what? Surely if the people repent and turn from their wickedness God will spare them, for such is His nature. He is gracious, compas-

sionate, long-suffering, and merciful. Before another charge comes I will run away and make it
physically impossible for me to fulfill this distasteful mission."

But more needs to be said about Jonah's motives
for his actions. Jonah, a superpatriot of Israel, had
appointed himself the defender of the faith. He
was irreverent in his concern and solicitude for
God's care of Israel. He had so identified himself
with God and Israel that he sincerely felt that the
cause of Jehovah would be better served by not
going on such an errand of mercy. As the Lord's
superzealot he was even willing to die. There is
something strangely amusing and at the same time
pathetic about his fanaticism.

Steeped in the narrow, carnal Jewish outlook of
the times, he actually felt he was defending God's
honor. He knew that Assyria was Israel's bitter enemy, and he could not reconcile himself to warning an enemy of God's wrath. The foe might take
heed and be saved, and Jonah was not willing to
undertake such a mission of mercy. So, to forestall
it, he fled. It is evident that Jonah had no love in
his heart for the Ninevites. And as we proceed it
becomes more and more obvious that the Lord
sought to open Jonah's eyes to this very fault.

Once we know why Jonah fled we are better able
to understand why he was so angry. The failure to

understand correctly his motive for running away in the first place has led to differences of opinion as to why he was angry over Nineveh's preservation. For example, some claim Jonah was angry because:

1. His experiences had brought him to the point of nervous exhaustion and extreme irritability.

2. The salvation of Nineveh meant the future destruction of Israel, and Jonah knew this.

3. Jonah's pride was hurt, his dignity offended. God had made a fool of him and he had become a laughingstock.

4. His reputation as a prophet was irreparably damaged. Surely he would be called a false prophet, a liar, a deceiver, and would be ridiculed and denounced for prophesying something which did not occur.

However, with all of these suggestions in mind it is best to conclude that since Jonah's rebellion at the first was the result of his mistaken and willful zeal, his anger at this stage was caused by the frustration of his own will.

Someone has said that *therefores* are there for a reason. In verse three the word *therefore* introduces Jonah's practical conclusion derived from his estimate of God's character. It is as if he said, "Since you have been so merciful, as I knew you

would be, and have spared Nineveh, then take
away my life."

Other men of God have also expressed despair
and a weariness of life. Moses became so disgusted
with the complaining and murmuring of the Israelites that he said to the Lord, "And if thou deal thus
with me, kill me, I pray thee, out of hand, if I have
found favor in thy sight (Exodus 11:15). Then
there was the prophet Elijah fleeing to Beersheba
before the wrath of Jezebel: "But he himself went
a day's journey into the wilderness, and came and
sat down under a juniper tree: and he requested
for himself that he might die, and said, It is enough;
now, O LORD, take away my life; for I am not better than my fathers" (I Kings 19:4). Job and Jeremiah also became weary of life, and lamented the
day they were born.

However, none of these men had the spirit of rebellion and self-will which gripped Jonah. Though
they seemed weary of life, they showed a spirit of
submissiveness. They yielded to the will of God.
They were somewhat like the Apostle Paul, in a
"strait betwixt two." But not Jonah. He was angry enough to die; his zeal was not tempered by
submissiveness. And yet he had enough presence
of mind to recognize that his life was in God's
hands, and that he was only a steward of the life
God had entrusted to him. Jonah was miserable

and as far as he was concerned, death was better for him than life.

There are two possible translations of verse 4: "Are you very angry?" or "Are you rightly angry?" The Septuagint supports the former rendering, but it does not seem to fit in well with the context. The latter translation seems better suited. The Lord was concerned with the rightness or ethical quality of Jonah's anger. The words "Doest thou well" are used adverbially here, but come from a verb meaning "to be good, well, glad, pleasing." The moral quality of Jonah's anger is the thing questioned.

God often asked men questions in order to help them see their own hearts. Consider Adam and Eve. Four questions were directed at them and these questions were calculated to make them aware of their faults: "Where art thou? . . . Who told thee that thou wast naked? Hast thou eaten of the tree, whereof I commanded thee that thou shouldest not eat? . . . What is this that thou has done?"

Cain was asked, "Where is Abel thy brother?" Of the prophet of fire, the Lord inquired, "What doest thou here, Elijah?" Of the archtraitor, Jesus asked, "Judas, betrayest thou the Son of man with a kiss?" To the impetuous Peter came the heartrending, thrice-repeated "Lovest thou me?" And, finally, to a stricken persecutor of the church came these words, "Saul, Saul, why persecutest thou me?"

In each instance the question was intended to pierce the heart of the hearer and lay bare his soul in some particular matter. And so it was with Jonah. The Lord desired Jonah to examine his behavior and see whether it was righteous or not. "Do you think that you are justly angry?" This was God's challenge to Jonah—to reflect whether his anger was justifiable or not. Here, Jehovah was not interested in the quantity or degree but rather in the quality of Jonah's anger.

The question obviously indicates the Lord's displeasure. But the reproof or correction of Jonah is really quite mild. In fact, the gentleness of God's rebuke favors the interpretation given earlier concerning Jonah's motives for running away. It appears that the Lord took into account Jonah's passionate desire for Israel's good and his wish to honor Jehovah's name. At this point we are reminded of the passion and zeal of Paul, who verily thought he "ought to do many things contrary to the name of Jesus of Nazareth" but obtained mercy because he did them ignorantly in unbelief. A man can be sincere—and wrong! And so, God dealt with Jonah accordingly.

B. *Reproof Prepared* (4:5-9)

So Jonah went out of the city, and sat on the east side of the city, and there made him a booth, and sat under it in the shadow, till he might see what would become of the city. And the Lord God prepared a gourd, and made it to come up over Jonah, that it might be a shadow over his head, to deliver him from his grief. So Jonah was exceeding glad of the gourd. But God prepared a worm when the morning rose the next day, and it smote the gourd that it withered. And it came to pass, when the sun did arise, that God prepared a vehement east wind; and the sun beat upon the head of Jonah, that he fainted, and wished in himself to die, and said, It is better for me to die than to live. And God said to Jonah, Doest thou well to be angry for the gourd? And he said, I do well to be angry, even unto death.

Because Jonah still justified his behavior, he did not answer the question. In anger he left to watch and see what would happen to Nineveh. Jonah's action here has caused wonderment. Some have suggested that the forty days had not expired, so the prophet had hopes that something evil might yet befall Nineveh. Another suggestion has been to translate "Jonah had gone" instead of "Jonah went out." However, the Hebrew grammar will not support this. Again, it has been asserted that this verse

(v. 5) should follow verse 4 of chapter 3. This would mean that after preaching, Jonah went outside of the city to a place of safety and remained there during the forty days. But this idea of transposing has little to support it.

It is true that we cannot be absolutely certain whether or not the forty days had expired, but in view of the fact that Jonah was so displeased, and even desired death, it would be natural to assume that he was convinced God would not destroy Nineveh *within* the forty-day period. We would suggest that the forty days were over at the time Jonah withdrew from the city. And since the probation period had ended, it probably occurred to him that perhaps the Lord would punish Nineveh later. Possibly, he thought, the Ninevites would rapidly fall into sin again, and their relapse into wickedness would call for an even worse punishment than that averted earlier!

Such thoughts would surely be in accord with what we know of Jonah. And so with this secret hope he waited. He built a booth and sat under its shade to observe. The booth was really like a thicket made of interwoven boughs and branches.

It is interesting to note that the word translated "grief" in verse 6 is generally translated evil or wickedness, as in Jonah 1:2. Elsewhere it is variously rendered "adversity, affliction, bad, calami-

ty, distress, harm, hurt, ill, mischief, misery, noi-
some, sad, sore, sorrow, trouble, vexation, wretchedness." The word combines the deed and the consequence of the deed. This would seem to indicate
that the word *grief* included not only Jonah's bad
attitude but the mental misery he felt also. The
Lord prepared the gourd and made it come up
over Jonah in order to alleviate his condition. Had
his grief been only mental, we would wonder how
the gourd helped.

Notice the word *displeased* in verse 1, chapter
4. It is related to the word which is translated
"grief." In other words, Jonah's displeasure was
his grief also. It was his own anger that made him
miserable. Isn't that the way it usually is?

Certainly there is the possibility of the spiritual
or mental condition being aggravated by the physical. Jonah was already "hot," and the sun's rays
probably helped to increase his distress. In light
of this we could say that the plant was designed by
God to afford the recalcitrant, disgruntled prophet
some measure of physical relief which in turn
would help to alleviate his mental distress.

The gourd is said to be the ricinus, or castor-
oil plant—a rapid-growing plant with huge, broad
leaves. Perhaps the foliage had withered on the
booth and no longer gave protection from the rays
of the sun. Or, to put it another way, the big leaves

of the gourd offered a better protective shadow than the booth alone.

The rapid manner in which the plant shot forth was supernatural. God had prepared it for the purpose of snatching Jonah away from his grief. And the strongly emotional prophet rejoiced.

In the Old Testament there are four different words which are translated "worm" in our King James Version. One word might more properly be translated "a moth" or "a larva of a moth." Another word means "a creeping crawling thing" or "a serpent." A third word indicates "corruption and decay." In Job 25:6, the worm is hyperbole for man's insignificance. In Exodus 16:24, the worms referred to were in the manna of the disobedient Israelites. All of the other scriptures using this third word refer to the grave or to human flesh. The worms in these verses are the maggots and larvae of insects which feed on putrifying matter.

The fourth word translated "worm" is found some 43 times and thus is the word most commonly used. Its root may mean "to gnaw." When combined with another Hebrew word meaning bright or scarlet, it speaks of the bright red female worm (*coccus ilicis*), whose dry body supplies coloring for cloth. The worm-dyed cloth called scarlet was symbolic of luxury. It was used as material for the curtains, veils, and ephods in the tabernacle, and in various rituals, sacrificial cleansings, and services.

In other places the worm symbolizes self-abasement, insignificance and wretchedness. God also used the worm as an instrument of judgment in punishing Israel for her disobedience. Isaiah spoke of the punishment of the wicked and declared, "Their worm shall not die, neither shall their fire be quenched" (Isa. 66:24). The Lord Jesus Christ repeated these words in Mark 9:44: "Where their worm dieth not, and the fire is not quenched." The voracious appetite of the worm is stressed here, and his gnawing and constant devouring symbolize the eternality of the punishment of the wicked. The worm that dieth not, then, is a figure of speech implying that one of the terrors of hell is the lack of a time limit to its torment!

The only other occurrence of the word *worm* in the New Testament also has to do with judgment. It concerns the death of King Herod Agrippa who, at the age of fifty-four, met an unpleasant death. According to the Scriptures, "he was eaten of worms, and gave up the ghost."

It should be obvious to the Bible reader that the Scriptures make no minute scientific distinctions as to the species of all these creatures. To the writers a worm was a worm, whether grub, earthworm, caterpillar, maggot, larva of a vine-weevil, or larvae of myriads of other insects. What does impress us is the fact that the Lord used such little things to carry out His great purposes. He is indeed the Lord of all nature. When He spoke, these creatures moved to do their duty. When He commanded, they performed their appointed tasks.

And through these lowly creatures men were taught the consequence of disobedience, reminded of their own insignificance, and impressed with the temporal nature of all things.

So it was that Jonah enjoyed for one day the overshadowing of the gourd. But at dawn of the day following, the Lord prepared the worm, and it gnawed and bored its way through the plant, causing it to dry up and die. Sometimes when the singular "worm" is used, it can be considered collectively as "worms." However, it is not necessary to do this in Jonah, for one worm could have done the job. Just as the growth of the prepared gourd was supernatural, so too its destruction by the prepared worm was miraculous.

The Hebrew word in verse 8 translated "vehement" is not found elsewhere in the Old Testament. Its real meaning is dubious and conjectures are numerous. Some suggested translations are: "autumn, burning, cutting, dry, silent, still." The Septuagint has rendered it the "scorching wind." Perhaps the best translation of the word is "sultry."

From the Arabic word meaning "east wind" comes the word *sirocco*. It is a hot, oppressive dust-laden wind that blows in from the desert or some other heated region. These siroccos may last from three days to a week at a time, and may occur any time from April to the middle of June, and from the middle of September to the end of October.

The destructive nature of the east wind is recorded in the Scriptures and is variously described as blasting, drying, scattering, shipwrecking, and wilting. It is also recorded how God used the east wind to execute judgment upon Egypt, the Chaldeans, the Ephraimites, and other disobedient people. On several occasions something beneficial was accomplished by the east wind: it divided the Red Sea for Israel and sent them manna and quail.

Jehovah had prepared a great fish to swallow Jonah, a gourd to overshadow him, a worm to destroy the gourd plant and, last, an east wind. The rapidity with which things are laid waste by the east wind reminds men of the ephemeral nature of material possessions and life itself. Combined with Jonah's disgust at the salvation of Nineveh, the east wind served to intensify his distress.

Notice that the sun beat upon the head of Jonah. The words "beat upon" come from the verb meaning "to smite," which in verse 7 is translated "smote." In other words, what the worm did to the gourd plant, the sun did to Jonah's head! The dehydration of the body, the burning of the eyes, the parching of the lips, and scorching of skin was too much. Jonah fainted!

We were amazed to discover some seventeen different Hebrew verbs translated "to faint." Some of them are used of physical feebleness, exhaustion, and weariness. Others are used figuratively and speak of timidity, fearfulness, despair, discouragement, sorrow, impatience, and distress of heart and mind.

The verb translated "fainted" in verse 8 is different from the one used in 2:7. Its root means to cover. In Song of Solomon 5:14, it is translated as "overlaid"; in Genesis 38:14, as "wrapped." The idea seems to be that a person who has swooned or fainted has his mind enshrouded, covered, or wrapped and his senses obscured.

The shelter of the plant had gone and the unbearable sultriness of the sirocco combined with the scorching sun rays to make Jonah literally "ask for his soul to die." That is, he wished for himself that he might die. As in verse 3, he again said, "Better my death than my life."

Note that in verse 9 God inquired the second time about the righteousness of Jonah's anger. The first time Jonah was angry as the result of the deliverance of the city of Nineveh. This time he was "burned up"—almost literally so—because of the gourd's destruction (and yet this anger too was indirectly connected with Nineveh's preservation). Jonah's distorted sense of values is clearly shown. He was more concerned with a plant than with people. God's question chided Jonah about this. When asked before whether his burning anger was justifiable, Jonah had not answered. But this time he answered, for his own personal comfort was involved. He asserted that he was rightly angry, even to the point of death, so great was his anger. The question had indeed probed Jonah's heart and sought the motive behind his anger. And the reply given was the means whereby God could put the prophet to shame.

C. *Lesson Taught* (4:10-11)

Then said the LORD, Thou hast had pity on the gourd, for the which thou hast not laboured, neither madest it grow; which came up in a night, and perished in a night: And should not I spare Nineveh, that great city, wherein are more than sixscore thousand persons that cannot discern between their right hand and their left hand; and also much cattle?

Jonah's selfishness had led him to look upon the gourd with compassion. It had sheltered him and brought him comfort and made him glad, and so

he was concerned about it. Not that it was his
gourd; no, he did not own it. He had no creative
powers and therefore had not brought the plant
into existence. Nor had he caused it to grow. And
yet—because it had afforded him shelter, he became
angry when it perished.

Jonah's affections had been misplaced, and the
Lord magnified Jonah's folly by informing him
that the gourd was "a son of a night and in a night
perished." The expression "son of a night" de-
scribes the transitory nature of the gourd. A son
of a night is only one night old, and for something
so short-lived, how could Jonah have so much compassion?

Jehovah's feeling is compared with Jonah's emotion. Actually the verb translated "had pity on"
(v. 10) is the same verb here translated "spare."
The Lord compared Jonah's compassion for the
gourd with His own compassion toward the people
of Nineveh. The contrast between Jehovah and
Jonah is further heightened by the use of emphatic
pronouns. In verse 10, "thou" is emphatic; in verse
11, "I" is emphatic. It is quite evident that God
desired Jonah to reflect upon the contrasts: Jehovah and Jonah, people and plant. Both comparisons—whether of those who showed mercy or of the
objects of their pity—point up the folly of Jonah's
attitude.

The prophet must realize that the city of Nineveh was no weed sprung up overnight but a great city. As determined earlier, it was not great in God's sight, but great to man's sight, and the Lord simply condescended to use this language of accommodation.

The exact number of persons present in the city at that time is unknown. Various population estimates are given and the differences of opinion are the result of the misinterpretation of the phrase "more than sixscore thousand persons that cannot discern their right hand from their left hand."

The original meaning of the word translated "right" is dubious. It may be connected with the verb "to conform" or "to support," from which the word *amen* is derived. It is quite possible that since most people are right-handed, that hand is the stronger of the two, and therefore the right hand was used in confirming an oath.

The root of the word translated "left" is also dubious. The left is connected with the north, which is on the left of a person facing the east. It is interesting to note that the same word translated "left" is rendered "north" in other versions of the Bible. The left is also considered unlucky or evil. It is interesting to note also that the word *sinister* is derived from the Latin word *sinistrum,* which means "evil, unlucky, inauspicious"; and the word *sinister* means *"left"* or *"on the left side."* All this stems from the fact that men believed that omens observed from one's left side were considered unlucky.

Thus it may be seen that the right hand stands for that which is effective and good. This meaning is seen in the following verses:

> A wise man's heart is at his right hand; but a fool's heart at his left (Eccles. 10:2).

> And he shall set the sheep on his right hand, but the goats on the left (Matt. 25:33).

Exactly what then does the inability to discern between the right hand and the left hand indicate? It means the inability to choose between good and evil, and therefore refers to spiritual ignorance and lack of moral discernment. Unfortunately, many commentators have concluded that the reference is to children who are incapable of distinguishing between their physical hands and therefore not able to tell the difference between good and bad. At what age this discernment develops is not known; consequently, scholars have differed in their estimations of the total population of Nineveh.

Some have suggested that they were infants under two years of age. We are then told that 120,000 innocent babies would indicate a population over two and a half million! Others put the age limit at seven and estimate the population at 600,000.

We reject altogether the belief that the 120,000 were all infants. Children are not the only ones spiritually ignorant. And, really, the comparison is not between an innocent plant and innocent children. Based upon our word study we would interpret this inability to discern between right and left hands as an indication of spiritual ignorance and lack of moral discernment. There is no reference to age.

Furthermore, the word translated "persons" is *adam*, which means "man" or "mankind." The word signifies human beings in general and nowhere refers exclusively to children or infants. In short, it does not appear that the Hebrew word *adam*, here translated as "persons" is ever used for children or babies. Therefore, we are not inclined to describe these 120,000 beings as children. They were all the human population who had not been aware of their own perilous plight or their own sad moral condition.

Next we see that the Lord's compassion embraced the cattle also. This is, physically speaking, still a step ahead of compassion for a plant. The word translated "cattle" means beast or animal, and our English word *behemoth* was derived from this Hebrew word translated cattle. God's concern for animals is amply taught in the Scriptures. Aside from what was stated earlier, we see that the Israelites were commanded by God not to work their beasts on the sabbath but to rest them. The ox that trod out the grain was not to be muzzled. Surely the Lord feeds and preserves and watches over the dumb creatures of the earth.

It has been suggested that the cattle were included because, like the 120,000 children, they too were innocent. However, we have seen that there is no basis for making "persons" children. It was not the Lord's purpose to stress innocence here but mercy—His mercy. Surely the people were more to be pitied than a plant! Why, even the cattle were to be pitied more!

So it was in this way that Jehovah sought to convince Jonah his zeal really had gone too far. Men who seek to thwart the will of God always act foolishly. Some are malicious in their attempts to frustrate God's purpose. These are wicked unsaved men. Others, like Jonah, are righteous, perhaps even self-righteous, and are overzealous. Jonah honestly, sincerely felt that God would best be glorified by the destruction of Nineveh. But the Lord will have mercy upon whom He desires, and no man can hinder Him.